Bf 110
vs
LANCASTER
1942–45

ROBERT FORCZYK

First published in Great Britain in 2013 by Osprey Publishing,
PO Box 883, Oxford, OX1 9PL, UK
1385 Broadway, 5th Floor, New York, NY 10018, USA
Email: info@ospreypublishing.com

Osprey Publishing is an imprint of Bloomsbury Publishing Plc

Transferred to digital print on demand 2016

First published 2013
2nd impression 2014

Printed and bound by PrintOnDemand-Worldwide.com, Peterborough, UK

A CIP catalogue record for this book is available from the British Library

ISBN: 978 1 78096 316 7
PDF eBook ISBN: 978 1 78096 317 4
ePub ISBN: 978 1 78096 318 1

Edited by Tony Holmes
Cover artworks and battlescene by Gareth Hector:
    www.garethhector.co.uk/aviation-art/
Three-views, cockpits, gunsight, armament scrap views and field-of-fire
    view by Jim Laurier
Index by Alan Thatcher
Originated by PDQ Digital Media Solutions, UK

The Woodland Trust

Osprey Publishing is supporting the Woodland Trust, the UK's leading
woodland conservation charity, by funding the dedication of trees.

www.ospreypublishing.com

Dedication

In remembrance of 1Lt Stephen C. Prasnicki, 4-319 FA (Abn)/173rd Airborne
Brigade Combat Team, who died of wounds caused by an IED attack in
Wardak Province, Afghanistan, on 27 June 2012.

Imperial War Museum Collections

Many of the photos in this book come from the Imperial War Museum's
huge collections which cover all aspects of conflict involving Britain and the
Commonwealth since the start of the 20th century. These rich resources are
available online to search, browse and buy at www.iwmcollections.org.uk. In
addition to Collections Online, you can visit the Visitor Rooms where you can
explore more than eight million photographs, thousands of hours of moving
images, the largest sound archive of its kind in the world, thousands of diaries
and letters written by people in wartime and a huge reference library. Imperial
War Museum www.iwm.org.uk

Bf 110 cover art

On the night of 21/22 January 1943, Feldwebel Theodor Kleinhenz, flying a
Bf 110F-4 nightfighter from III./NJG 1, took off from Leeuwarden airfield, in
the Netherlands, and headed for his assigned patrol area. The aircraft carried a
FuG 202 *Lichtenstein* B/C radar, operated by Unteroffizier Hermann Gempe.
Shortly thereafter, German ground-based radar detected British bombers
flying across Holland, en route to Essen, and Kleinhenz was vectored to
intercept them. At a range of about 1,000m, Gempe detected a bomber
ahead of them. It was Lancaster B I W4335/PM-F from No. 103 Sqn,
flown by Sgt Edward V. Laing (RAAF). Kleinhenz closed the distance and
fired several cannon bursts into the rear of the Lancaster. Seconds later the
bomber burst into flames as its port wing tank caught fire. The Lancaster
crashed at 1935 hrs near Enschede, killing all seven crew members. Kleinhenz,
who reported seeing no return fire from the rear gunner, was later shot down
and killed over Rumania in April 1944, but Gempe survived the war.
(Artwork by Gareth Hector)

Lancaster cover art

Lancaster B III ND911/V-JN from No. 75 'New Zealand' Sqn, flown by
Plt Off Patrick L. McCartin, is illuminated by the raging fires of a burning
Cologne on the night of 31 October 1944. The bomber is being stalked by
a Bf 110G-4 nightfighter from IV./NJG 1, its pilot attempting to set up a
Schräge Musik attack. Bf 110 crews usually tried to avoid interceptions over
cities since there was danger from flak and too much light, revealing their
presence to the bomber gunners, but some would take the risk in order to
achieve surprise against unwary Lancaster crews. However, Lancaster
ND911 had already survived 70 operational missions over Europe by
31 October 1944, and McCartin managed to avoid the attack. Unfortunately,
his luck ran out three weeks later when ND911 was shot down by flak over
Homberg. Only one crewmember of the seven on board survived. (Artwork
by Gareth Hector with thanks to Piotr Forkasiewicz for the use of his
Lancaster model)

CONTENTS

INTRODUCTION

'the bomber will always get through . . .'
British Prime Minister Stanley Baldwin, 10 November 1932

The British people had discovered first hand during World War I that night-bombing was a terrifying experience, and very difficult to defend against. For three years, German Zeppelins and Gotha bombers conducted strategic bombing raids over England, killing 1,413 civilians. Britain's leadership believed that bombing seriously undermined civilian morale, and noted the difficulty their fighters had in intercepting German bombers. After World War I, Air Marshal (AM) Sir Hugh Trenchard, first commander of the Royal Air Force (RAF), regarded strategic bombing as a preferred alternative to costly battles of attrition on the ground, and pushed the Air Ministry to support the development of heavy bombers.

In pursuit of this objective, the RAF formed Bomber Command in July 1936, which was viewed as a deterrent to German aggression and, if necessary, an economical means of conducting strategic warfare. Opinions within the Air Ministry differed on whether a bomber force was best used in massed daylight raids or in more dispersed attacks at night, but the basic efficacy of strategic bombing was not questioned.

It was widely believed that neither fighters nor flak defences could stop bombers from reaching their targets, even though umpires in a simulated RAF attack on London in 1931 judged that 84 of 112 bombers involved were destroyed. Practical factors, such as the difficulty of long-range navigation at night or the ability of enemy defences to disrupt bombing raids, were conveniently ignored. Indeed, RAF Bomber Command and Britain's political leadership developed an intrinsic faith in the capabilities of strategic bombing while avoiding realistic training in peacetime exercises, partly because this could be quite costly. Only five months after the creation of Bomber Command, seven Handley Page Heyford bombers took off on a long-distance night exercise but four crashed due to poor weather. These were seen as quite unacceptable losses in peacetime training. Thereafter, night training was limited.

Nevertheless, the RAF leadership continued to glibly espouse the theory of strategic night bombing during the 1930s, while committing minimal resources towards night training or the development of electronic navigation aids that could transform this idea into a practical warfighting doctrine. Instead, the Air Ministry put its faith in developing bigger bombers, better bombers and more bombers, particularly a new generation of four-engined heavy bombers.

On the other side of the hill, the Luftwaffe, headed by *Reichsmarschall* Hermann Göring, was equally enamoured with developing a bomber force, but for aggression, not deterrence. Luftwaffe leaders were also interested in night operations, and began modifying commercially available radio navigation technology into a system for blind-bombing. When war came, the Luftwaffe had the *Knickebein* system and was close to perfecting the *X-Gerät*, making its bombers far more capable of night bombing than Bomber Command.

However, the German leadership expected a short war, and did not anticipate significant enemy bombing of German cities. Göring reckoned that if enemy bombers did attack German territory at night, existing flak and searchlight units would be adequate to disrupt raids. Publicly, Göring was against 'wasting' resources in creating a specialised nightfighter force when the threat appeared hypothetical, and openly declared that the Luftwaffe would never need a nightfighter unit. Yet Göring was less sanguine in private, and quietly authorised the *Reichsluftfahrtministerium* (Air Ministry [RLM]) to work with the German electronics industry to develop and test new technology that could assist the Luftwaffe with nightfighting.

Two major Berlin-based companies, Allgemeine Elektricitäts-Gesellschaft (AEG) and Siemens, as well as their joint subsidiary Telefunken, were encouraged to develop electronic and infrared (IR) detection equipment. Both companies had provided substantial financial support to the Nazis during their rise to power, and enjoyed close personal ties with Göring himself.

A Bf 110C from II./ZG 76 in 1940. The aircraft had been developed as both a heavy, long-range fighter and a bomber destroyer (*Zerstörer*), but it failed miserably in this role against RAF single-engined fighters in the Battle of Britain. When surviving Bf 110s were assigned to the first *Nachtjagd* units, both the RAF and the Luftwaffe believed that this aircraft's career was virtually over. Both sides were wrong. (Bundesarchiv, Bild 101I-382-0211-011, Foto: Benno Wundshammer)

When the war started in September 1939, RAF Bomber Command had a force of 349 twin-engined medium bombers (Wellingtons, Whitleys, Hampdens and Blenheims), which lacked the range and payload for an effective strategic bombing campaign over Germany. Given the difficulty of night operations, and its untested faith in the defensive firepower of tight bomber formations, Bomber Command initially mounted several daylight raids against German naval shipping. However, the RAF quickly discovered that unescorted bombers suffered unacceptable losses from enemy fighters. During the Battle of Heligoland Bight on 18 December 1939, ten of the 22 attacking Wellington bombers were shot down by Luftwaffe Bf 109 and Bf 110 day fighters. This brief air battle had a profound effect on both sides. RAF leaders decided to shift their emphasis towards night bombing, although Bomber Command never completely transitioned to night operations and continually experimented with daylight operations when it thought conditions were favourable. The Luftwaffe leadership gained an appreciation for the value of early warning radar since two of its new Telefunken-designed *Freya* radars had contributed to the victory over Heligoland Bight. Consequently, Göring authorised a much larger investment in Telefunken's radar development projects.

During 1940, Bomber Command conducted 20,809 sorties, of which 84 per cent occurred at night. However, RAF bombing was spread across a large number of naval and industrial targets, and was so woefully inaccurate that it contributed very little towards the defeat of Germany. Bomber Command's lack of prior investment in night navigation technology deprived it of the means of even finding large, blacked-out German cities at night. In one pathetic case, a Whitley bomber on a night mission mistakenly bombed an RAF fighter base in England when its crew thought that they were over Holland. In contrast, German bombers employing *Knickebein* and *X-Gerät* were capable of precision night bombing, and they caused more than 13,000 civilian fatalities in England just in September-October 1940. In retaliation, Prime Minister Winston Churchill directed the Air Ministry to authorise a policy of area bombing on 30 October 1940, which set the pattern for Bomber Command for the rest of the war.

Although British night bombing of German cities was initially little more than a nuisance, Göring was forced for prestige reasons to increase the Luftwaffe's ability to counter the nocturnal raiders. Consequently, in July 1940 Göring picked Oberst Josef Kammhuber to head the Luftwaffe's first real nightfighter command, 1. *Nachtjagddivision*, which was created to direct the newly-formed *Nachtjagdgeschwader* 1 (NJG 1). The latter was initially comprised of two *gruppen* with 72 Bf 110C twin-engined fighters. It is important to note that when NJG 1 was formed, the Bf 110 had not yet suffered heavy losses in the Battle of Britain, and its reputation was still intact. Soon thereafter, a Bf 110C from NJG 1 achieved the Luftwaffe's first true night victory on 22 July by shooting down a Whitley bomber. In September, a second *Nachtjagd* unit, NJG 2, was stood up and equipped with Ju 88C and Do 17 aircraft.

Nevertheless, the lack of radar detection equipment made it difficult for nightfighter crews to intercept British bombers. Indeed, Kammhuber's fighters only succeeded in shooting down 41 RAF bombers in 1940, of which 19 were claimed by Bf 110s – eight of these kills were credited to one Bf 110 pilot. Initially, Kammhuber's crews relied on 'illumination tactics' by attacking bombers that were spotlighted by Luftwaffe searchlight units on the ground, but this meant that the Bf 110C *Nachtjagd* in 1940 were really only capable of point defence of cities.

Bomber Command realised that only 12 per cent of its losses were due to enemy nightfighters, and regarded flak as the primary threat. Both sides drew conclusions from night operations in 1940 – the Luftwaffe that radar was essential to improving the ability of the *Nachtjagd* to detect and attack raiders, and the RAF that the defensive capability of its bombers was adequate against a minimal nightfighter threat.

In 1941 the RAF increased its strategic bombing campaign on Germany, flying 27,101 night sorties. Unable to conduct ground operations on the European continent, Prime Minister Winston Churchill saw Bomber Command's strategic bombing campaign as the only readily-available means of inflicting damage on the Third Reich, and lavished an estimated one-third of Britain's industrial resources on building up the RAF's bomber fleet. With great anticipation, Bomber Command began to field its first heavy bombers in February 1941 with the Short Stirling, followed by the Handley Page Halifax and Avro Manchester in March 1941. Deliveries of the first Avro Lancasters would not begin until December. However, the number of heavy bombers available throughout 1941 was less than one-quarter of Bomber Command's frontline strength, and the bombing offensive continued to rely upon the twin-engined Wellington until 1943.

British night raids remained fairly small throughout 1941, rarely exceeding 150 aircraft, and limited to small bomb-loads against peripheral targets in the Ruhr and on the German coast. Bomber Command could not strike heavy blows against Berlin or other key German cities in the heartland of the Third Reich until it had sufficient heavy bombers. Yet its losses slowly crept upward to a 2.5 per cent sortie-loss rate as German defences improved – of the 698 night bombers lost in 1941, the *Nachtjagd* claimed 425 kills, including 198 by Bf 110s. Given Churchill's commitment to provide Bomber Command with thousands of new four-engined bombers, RAF leaders believed that a 2.5 per cent loss rate was acceptable. They also believed that once the new heavy bombers – particularly the Lancaster – were available in quantity

The Avro Lancaster began active operations with the RAF in March 1942 after a five-year development programme. Bomber Command believed that four-engined heavy bombers like the Lancaster (these examples are from No. 44 "Rhodesia" Sqn) were capable of inflicting a crippling blow upon the Third Reich. (Imperial War Museum, TR198)

from 1942, the RAF would finally have the war-winning weapon system that had been envisioned by bomber enthusiasts for two decades.

However, Bomber Command did not count on the level of ingenuity displayed by the Luftwaffe. Faced with a British bomber offensive that was unprecedented in scale, Göring promoted Kammhuber to Generalmajor and expanded his command into XII. *Fliegerkorps* in August 1941. Empowered with greater authority, Kammhuber began creating the first Integrated Air Defence System (IADS) that coordinated his fighters with radar, searchlight and flak units.

Gradually, a line of *Freya* and *Würzburg* radars were deployed along the western border of Germany and the Low Countries that the RAF dubbed the 'Kammhuber Line'. This line provided a means for the *Nachtjagd* to detect and engage British night bombers. A real nightfighter, the Bf 110F-4 with the FuG 202 Lichtenstein aerial intercept (AI) radar, was introduced in August 1941, providing Kammhuber with the means for his fighters to find and attack targets beyond the searchlight zones. By late 1941, Kammhuber had also gained another Bf 110-equipped unit, NJG 3, which increased his *Nachtjagd* force to a total of 187 nightfighters.

At the start of 1942, Bomber Command was girding itself to inflict the first powerful doses of sustained aerial bombardment upon German cities, delivered by the latest heavy bombers and guided to targets by new radio navigation techniques. However, Kammhuber's nightfighters were no longer toothless, the *Nachtjagd* rapidly evolving into an elite and lethal force.

The aerial duel over Western Europe between the Lancaster and the Bf 110 nightfighter would extend over the next three years, and determine the efficacy of Britain's strategic

Wearing a kapok-filled aircrew lifejacket, the pilot of Bf 110C 'C5+DT' of 9./NJG 3 climbs aboard his aircraft at the start of yet another mission in the early autumn of 1941. This machine still bears the distinctive 'sharksmouth' marking of II./ZG 76, which supplied early *Nachtjagd* units with many of their Bf 110s. (via Jerry Scutts)

The FN 20 rear turret had amazingly poor visibility due to its large Plexiglas panels, designed to protect the gunner from biting winds at high altitude. The rear gunner was forced to search for enemy nightfighters through a narrow upper panel. Captured Bf 110 pilots noted that 80 per cent of Lancaster rear gunners did not return fire when approached – they often could not see the Bf 110 that was attacking them. (Imperial War Museum, TR 187)

Luftwaffe 'black men' (armourers, radio technicians, airframe repair teams and other specialists) were an integral part of every *Nachtjagd* unit. Here, armourers prepare to work on the quartet of 7.92mm Rheinmetall MG 17s mounted in the nose of a Bf 110C of 4./NJG 1. (via Jerry Scutts)

bombing campaign. Yet unlike other aircraft duels, the tactical contest between the Lancaster and the Bf 110 was not determined by simple factors such as aerodynamics, engineering or weapons. Rather, the duel between Lancasters and Bf 110s was shaped by a hide-and-seek dynamic, with the fighters attempting to find the bombers in a pitch dark sky. Scientists were also heavily involved in this duel in the darkness. Victory would go to the side that made the best use of cutting-edge technology to 'see' the enemy's aircraft while blinding the enemy's own sensors.

CHRONOLOGY

1934
June   German RLM issues a requirement for a twin-engined heavy fighter.

1935
January   RAF introduces power-operated gun turrets with the delivery of the Boulton Paul Overstrand to No. 101 Sqn.
1 March   Luftwaffe officially established.
Spring   German firm GEMA GmbH achieves breakthrough in radar technology and patents first cavity magnetron.

1936
12 May   First flight of the Bf 110 V1 prototype.
July   Air Ministry issues Specification B.12/36 for a new four-engined heavy bomber.
14 July   RAF Bomber Command formed.
24 August   Specification P.13/36 issued.
8 September   Air Ministry orders two prototypes of the Avro 679 (Manchester).
December   Göring orders the RLM to authorise production of the Bf 110 and 12 *Freya* radars.

1937
July   Air Ministry orders 200 Avro 679 bombers.
August   Bf 110A pre-production model begins testing.

1939
January   Luftwaffe receives first Bf 110C production models.

18 December   Battle of the Heligoland Bight sees the first detection and interception of RAF bombers directed by *Freya* EW radar. RAF duly switches to night bombing.

1940
April   RLM issues a requirement for a radar for nightfighters. Telefunken begins developing Lichtenstein radar.
22 June   Luftwaffe forms NJG 1 with Bf 110Cs.
4 July   Rolls-Royce introduces the Merlin XX engine.
20 July   First German nightfighter victory of the war by 2./NJG 1 over a Whitley.
10 September   First Avro Lancaster prototype ordered.
October   First *Himmelbett* radar station operational.
November   Avro Manchester enters service with No. 207 Sqn.

1941
9 January   First flight of the Lancaster prototype.
July   Telefunken GmbH begins testing FuG 202 *Lichtenstein* B/C aerial radar.
8/9 August   First kill by a *Lichtenstein*-equipped nightfighter.

Bf 110D fighters under construction in 1940. In contrast to the British emphasis on rapidly ramping up Lancaster production, Bf 110 production dropped off sharply after June 1941, and was briefly terminated in December 1941. Even after production was resumed in February 1942, construction of Bf 110 nightfighters remained a low priority for the Luftwaffe. (Author)

Autumn	Oberleutnant Rudolf Schoenert of 4./NJG 2 begins experimenting with upward-firing guns.
31 October	First production Lancaster completed.
24 December	No. 44 Sqn receives two Lancasters.
December	RLM halts Bf 110 production.

1942

22 February	Air Chief Marshal (ACM) Arthur Harris takes over Bomber Command.
March	Bf 110Es of I./NJG 1 begin receiving FuG 202 *Lichtenstein* B/C airborne radar.
March	Bf 110 production resumes.
March	British test *Window* in secret.
10 March	First Lancaster mission over Germany flown by No. 44 Sqn.
30/31 May	First use of bomber stream by RAF in Cologne raid.
June	Bf 110G pre-production model begins flight testing.
3 June	First Lancaster shot down by a Bf 110 nightfighter from NJG 1.
24 June	Manchester retired from Bomber Command service.
September	German *Freya* radar begins switching to variable frequencies (2.3-2.5m).
December	RAF begins using *Mandrel* to jam *Freya* radar.

1943

30 January	RAF bombers begin using H2S ground-mapping radar (10cm).
March	Bf 110G-4 enters operational use.
May	British acquire an intact FuG 202 radar.
June	*Monica* tail-warning radar detection device introduced on Lancasters.
24-25 July	First RAF use of *Window* during Hamburg raid.
17/18 August	Peenemünde raid. Bf 110G-4s with *Schräge Musik* shoot down five Lancasters.
September	Improved FuG 220 *Lichtenstein* SN-2 radar introduced.
13 October	Lancaster Airborne Cigar (ABC) jammers introduced.
November	*Fishpond* radar warning device introduced on H2S-equipped Lancasters.
November	No. 100 Group radar countermeasures sorties begin in an effort to jam *Nachtjäger* communications.
16 December	Mosquito *Serrate* missions begin targeting Bf 110 nightfighters.
December	British intelligence gets first report about *Schräge Musik* from a PoW interrogation.

1944

30-31 March	64 Lancasters shot down during the Nurnberg raid.
May	Rose turret introduced on aircraft of selected Lancaster squadrons.
21 May	A Bf 110G-4 equipped with SN-2 radar and *Schräge Musik* lands in Switzerland.
July	FN 121 Automatic Gun-Laying Turret (AGLT) fitted to selected Lancasters.
September	*Monica* abandoned.
October	RAF introduces *Dinah* to jam SN-2 radar.

1945

21 February	Heinz-Wolfgang Schnaufer uses *Schräge Musik* to shoot down seven Lancasters, thus giving the Bf 110 its final major success.

Lancaster bombers under construction at the A. V. Roe Woodford facility near Manchester. Each bomber required about 75,000 man hours to construct, and by July 1943 A. V. Roe had three plants producing a total of 160 Lancasters per month (each once costing approximately £42,000). Peak production was not reached until September 1944. (Imperial War Museum, TR 1386)

DESIGN AND DEVELOPMENT

'It was necessary that our aeroplanes should have the maximum offensive power in a European War.'
Gp Capt Arthur Harris, 1936

LANCASTER

Despite severe cutbacks in military expenditures after World War I, the RAF managed to find the resources to build up a force of more than 200 biplane bombers in the 1920s. AM Hugh Trenchard, Chief of the Air Staff, was committed to the theory of strategic bombing and favoured the development of both day and night bombers. However, Trenchard's bombers were designed in an era when the RAF leaders believed that a bomber was 'heavy' if it could haul two to three 500lb bombs far as Paris, not Berlin.

In August 1927, the Air Ministry's Specification B.19/27 called for a heavy bomber capable of night operations and able to deliver a 1,546lb bomb load to a range of 920 miles. The result was Britain's last biplane bomber, the Handley Page Heyford, which entered service in 1933. A year later, the RAF introduced power-operated gun turrets. These were widely believed to make bombers virtually invulnerable to opposing fighters, most of which were armed with just two light machine guns. Yet both aviation technology and international politics evolved very rapidly in the 1930s, and even before Hitler's decision to form the Luftwaffe, the Air Ministry recognised that the Heyford was obsolete upon delivery and should be replaced by a new generation of all-metal monoplane bombers. Between 1932 and 1934, the Air Ministry issued specifications for new twin-engined monoplane medium and heavy bombers, which soon resulted in orders for the Armstrong Whitworth Whitley, Handley Page Hampden and Vickers Wellington. In developing the desired characteristics for the new generation of bombers, the Air Ministry's Directorate of Operational Requirements placed particular emphasis on speed, large bomb-loads and long range, but neglected defensive armament.

The Air Ministry was still struggling with the distinctions between light, medium and heavy bombers, and the resulting specifications issued to industry were often muddled compromises. Furthermore, Britain's commitment to the League of Nations' World Disarmament Conference in Geneva, which attempted to abolish heavy bombers by imposing weight limits upon new designs, severely restricted the RAF's development of its first-generation monoplane bombers. It was not until Germany withdrew from the League in October 1933 and the collapse of the Geneva talks the next year that the political restrictions upon RAF bomber development were lifted. Interestingly, had Hitler kept Germany in the League of Nations a few more years, the Lancaster might not have been ready in time to participate in World War II.

Once the Geneva restrictions were removed and Britain embarked upon a rearmament programme, the Air Ministry revised Specification B.9/32 to increase the size and capabilities of the Hampden and the Wellington, but this would delay their entry into service until 1938. As a quick fix, the Air Ministry issued Specification B.1/35 in May 1935 and awarded contracts to Vickers and Handley Page to develop improved medium bombers. However the Whitley's design, which was deemed to be unsuited to upgrading, was left unaltered so that the RAF could begin receiving at least one new bomber in 1937. As it was increasingly realised that Germany was becoming a threat, the Air Ministry recognised that the Hampden and Wellington could not deliver adequate bomb loads to distant targets such as Berlin. Consequently, the Air Ministry was obliged in 1935 to begin developing a new set of specifications for a second-generation of monoplane medium and heavy bombers that would have the range and payload to conduct strategic bombing operations across central Europe. In particular, Gp Capt Arthur Harris, Deputy Director of Operations in the Air Ministry, argued that the RAF would require bombers with a range of at least 2,000 miles. Others in the Air Ministry advocated larger bomb loads, greater speed and enhanced armament, which was difficult to reconcile all in one design.

Although a four-engined bomber seemed to offer the best combination of capabilities, there was considerable disagreement within the Air Staff about whether bombers this large were necessary. Air Commodore Reynell H. Verney, Director of Technical Development, argued that four-engined bombers would be too expensive. In order to keep the new bomber force economical, the RAF's leadership favoured a single new bomber that was capable of dual-purpose day/night operations, as well as secondary roles, such as reconnaissance, transport or torpedo-bombing.

LANCASTER B I

69ft 6in.

102ft 0in.

Specification	Date of Issue	Bomb Load (lbs)	Range (miles)	Aircraft Ordered	Cost per Aircraft
B.9/32	September 1932	1,000 (1932)	600 (1932)	Hampden	£10,571
		2,000 (1934)	720 (1934)	Wellington	£14,367
B.3./34	July 1934	1,500	1,250	Whitley	£11,160
B.1/35	May 1935	2,000	1,500	HP 55 Warwick	-
B.12/36	July 1936	14,000	2,000	Stirling	£23,490
		8,000	3,000		
P.13/36	August 1936	3,600	3,000	HP 56/ Halifax	£23,354
		8,000 (overload)	1,800	Manchester	£36,812

Unfortunately, the Air Staff could not reconcile its differences, and decided to develop separate requirements for new medium and heavy bombers. In order to meet the conflicting requirements of range, bomb load and speed, as well as limiting cost for each aircraft, Verney recommended that an untried scheme for catapult-launched bombers be offered as a solution. He argued that by designing bombers that could be launched by catapult, the aircraft could be over-loaded with heavier bomb loads than they could normally takeoff with, and obviate the need for four engines. Despite the fact that Verney's catapult idea was untested, it was incorporated as a requirement into the Air Ministry's plans for a new heavy and medium bomber. It should be noted that aside from Harris, most senior members of the Air Staff involved in shaping the requirements for the new bombers had little or no direct experience with aircraft of this type, and no technical training. In July 1936, the staff issued Specification B.12/36 for a four-engined heavy bomber, which was expected to carry a maximum bomb load of 14,000lb to a range of 2,000 miles, or an 8,000lb bomb load up to 3,000 miles. Specification B.12/36 sought a revolutionary leap forward in bomber technology, representing a three-fold increase in range and payload capabilities over existing bombers.

Surprisingly, there were no less than seven contenders for the requirement, with Vickers and Supermarine being favoured by the Air Ministry. However, members of its Operational Requirements branch became besotted with an unsolicited bid from Short Brothers, who claimed that they could quickly develop a heavy bomber prototype from its four-engined S 25 flying boat. After waiting a year for the Supermarine design, the Air Ministry finally awarded the contract to Short Brothers in October 1937. The direct result of Specification B.12/36 was the Stirling, Britain's first four-engined heavy bomber, which made its initial flight four months before the beginning of World War II.

While authorising the development of a four-engined heavy bomber, the Air Ministry also wanted to develop a new twin-engined medium bomber with enhanced capabilities. Some members of the Air Staff were suspicious that their government might attempt to use the four-engined heavy bomber as a bargaining chip in renewed

OPPOSITE
Built at the Mosley Road Works in Manchester, Lancaster B I R5868 was delivered to No. 83 Sqn at Scampton on 29 June 1942. The aircraft proved to be very lucky, as it was attacked by nightfighters on several occasions – including by a Bf 110 over Berlin on 29/30 March 1943. In September 1943 R5868 was transferred to No. 467 Sqn, Royal Australian Air Force, based at Bottesford. Here, it was given the code letters 'PO-S' ('S for Sugar'). Moving with the squadron to Waddington on 11 November 1943, the bomber was fitted with H2S radar in November 1944. R5868 is seen here as it appeared in December 1944, when it had been recoded 'Q for Queenie'. On 23 April 1945 the Lancaster performed its 137th, and last, combat mission, to Flensberg, but it did not drop its bombs as Allied forces had occupied the city. Now at the end of an outstanding operational career, during which it had dropped 466 tons of ordnance, R5868 was flown to Wroughton, where it was placed in storage until struck off charge on 16 March 1956. Three years later it was moved to Scampton for service as a gate guardian. On 24 November 1970, R5868 was dismantled and removed to Bicester for refurbishment. On 12 March 1972, the bomber was moved to the RAF Museum at Hendon, in London, where it can be seen on display today as the centrepiece of the Bomber Command Hall.

Avro developed the twin-engined Manchester bomber to satisfy the Air Ministry's Specification P.13/36 issued in August 1936. In order to meet the ministry's requirement for a twin-engined bomber that could carry a heavy bomb payload, Avro designed the Manchester to withstand the stress of a catapult launch. Although this requirement was dropped, it led to a very sturdy design in the form of the later Lancaster bomber. (Author)

arms control negotiations with Germany, and therefore they did not want to rely entirely upon one aircraft to meet all their strategic bombing requirements. Specification P.13/36 was issued in August 1936, calling for a twin-engined medium bomber for 'worldwide' use, although this was disingenuous, since the P.13/36 was primarily intended for operations against Germany. The Air Ministry wanted the P.13/36 bomber to carry 3,600lb of bombs up to 3,000 miles or – with catapult assistance – 8,000lb of bombs up to 1,800 miles. In addition to Verney's catapult-launch requirement, the Air Staff tacked on additional requirements that the aircraft should be capable of dive-bombing and launching 18-in. torpedoes, which were more than 16ft long and weighed 1,500lb. Although these last two requirements were subsequently dropped, they did greatly influence the design of the P.13/36 bomber.

The main contenders for Specification P.13/36 were Handley Page, Vickers and Avro. Handley Page was already developing the HP 55 to meet Specification B.1/35 and Vickers was developing the Warwick, an improved variant of the Wellington. Avro was a different story.

The company, originally Alliott Verdon-Roe, had made its name creating trainers for the RAF. Avro's chief designer, the talented Roy Chadwick, had been creating

Roy Chadwick, designer of the Lancaster bomber, with Wg Cdr Guy Gibson. Chadwick was one of the most talented British aircraft designers of the 1930s, and he also contributed to the design of the post-war Avro Vulcan bomber. (Author)

fighters and bombers for 25 years, although few had been ordered by the RAF. When Specification P.13/36 appeared, most of the other large aircraft manufacturers were focused on Specification B.12/36 for the heavy bomber, providing Avro with a window of opportunity to compete for this work. Fortuitously, Chadwick had in hand a design known as the Avro 679, which the Air Ministry found attractive. Normally, the Air Ministry would have held a formal competition and then selected just one design to meet its requirement, but since the RAF's budget nearly doubled in 1937 the Air Ministry placed an order for three prototypes – two Avro 679s and one Handley Page HP 56.

The Manchester bomber was plagued by its unreliable Rolls-Royce Vulture engines, which over-heated and had poor operational reliability. Despite Chadwick's best efforts the Manchester remained unsatisfactory, and the Lancaster was developed as a four-engined alternative. (Imperial War Museum, CH3879)

Yet ministry officials were so anxious to increase the size of Bomber Command to counter political allegations that the RAF was inferior to the new Luftwaffe that they decided not to wait for the prototypes to be built or tested. In July 1937 the Air Ministry placed an order for 200 Avro 679s and 100 HP 56 bombers. Eventually, these aircraft would enter RAF service as the Avro Manchester and the Handley Page Halifax. It is also important to note that RAF bombers became significantly more complex and expensive in just a few years. While the Whitleys bought for the RAF averaged out at £11,000 apiece and the Wellingtons £14,000, the Stirlings and Halifaxes cost £23,000 each and the Manchester £36,800.

During this period, the question of improving defensive armament for bombers to match the increased firepower of fighters was raised, and Sir Edward Ellington, head of the Air Ministry, asked if 0.50in. heavy machine guns or 20mm cannons could be mounted in turrets fitted in the new heavy and medium bombers. Expending negligible effort, Ellington's staff assured him that 0.303in. machine guns in turrets were still adequate as defensive armament on bombers, and that the use of larger weapons was unnecessary. Yet, in 1938, the Air Staff changed its mind and advocated improved defensive weaponry on bombers, but by this point it was too late to make major changes without pushing delivery dates even further back. This tendency by technically illiterate members of the Air Staff towards snap decisions on selection and development of new aircraft designs would have a profound effect on the duel between British bombers and German nightfighters in the next war.

In order to satisfy Specification P.13/36's torpedo requirement, Chadwick realised that he would have to build the Avro 679 around an enormous, 33ft long bomb-bay. In contrast, the Stirling had a 42ft long, divided, bomb-bay and the HP 56 bomber a 22ft long bomb-bay. However, getting the 15.6-ton Avro 679 into the air with only two engines would require motors with considerably more horsepower than those fitted to previous RAF bombers. Realising this, the Air Ministry stated that both Avro and

The Manchester first entered RAF service in November 1940, and the bomber flew its first mission over Germany in March 1941. Of the 202 built by Avro, 69 were lost on operations and 53 crashed. No more than 20 were ever available for frontline service at any one time, and the type was retired in June 1942 once Lancaster production got into its stride. (Imperial War Museum, HU 42453)

A Fraser-Nash FN 4 rear gun turret, fitted with four 0.303in. Browning machine guns, on a Manchester bomber. Bomber Command was very impressed with the hydraulically-powered gun turrets developed in the 1930s, but weak defensive armament ultimately proved to be the Achilles heel of the Lancaster. (Imperial War Museum, CH 17292)

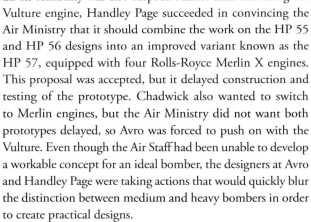

Handley Page should use the new Rolls-Royce Vulture engines on their prototypes. Rolls-Royce claimed that its Vulture, which had just entered production in 1936, offered very high power output, and this impressed the Air Ministry. In fact, the Vulture engine had a host of technical problems, foremost of which was that it did not deliver the promised power output. Its reliability was also suspect. Rather than risk using the Vulture engine, Handley Page succeeded in convincing the Air Ministry that it should combine the work on the HP 55 and HP 56 designs into an improved variant known as the HP 57, equipped with four Rolls-Royce Merlin X engines. This proposal was accepted, but it delayed construction and testing of the prototype. Chadwick also wanted to switch to Merlin engines, but the Air Ministry did not want both prototypes delayed, so Avro was forced to push on with the Vulture. Even though the Air Staff had been unable to develop a workable concept for an ideal bomber, the designers at Avro and Handley Page were taking actions that would quickly blur the distinction between medium and heavy bombers in order to create practical designs.

Despite having gained an edge over Handley Page by sticking with the problematic Vulture engine, it took Avro two full years to design and construct the Avro 679 prototype, which did not make its first flight until 25 July 1939 – just two months ahead of the four-engined HP 57 prototype. Flight testing quickly confirmed some of the fears about the unreliability of the Vulture engines, which were prone to overheating and produced less power output than had been expected. The engines were also one ton overweight, which seriously degraded the Avro 679's speed. Instability issues forced Chadwick to lengthen the Avro 679's wingspan from 80ft to 90ft and to modify the tail. Nevertheless, flight testing was plagued by problems, and in December 1939 the Avro 679 prototype crashed as a result of engine failure.

The Air Ministry recognised that the Avro 679, now designated the Manchester, was unsatisfactory, but since World War II had by now begun it would not abandon the project. Instead, the order for Manchester bombers was increased to 1,200! While Avro was satisfied with the procurement contracts, Chadwick was not satisfied with the Manchester, and even before the loss of the first prototype he had ordered some of his engineering staff to begin designing a four-engined variant, designated the Type 683 or Manchester III, as insurance.

Chadwick's follow-on design used the Manchester's fuselage and centre-wing sections, thus achieving 70 per cent commonality with the Avro 679. The main change for the new aircraft was the further lengthening of the wingspan to 100ft to accommodate four instead of two engines. Meanwhile, Avro established a production line for the Manchester

bomber at its Newton Heath facility near Manchester, and a modified Manchester prototype was completed in May 1940. The second series of flight tests demonstrated somewhat improved performance, so Avro finalised the design and prepared for limited series production in August.

Everything changed after the fall of France, however. Churchill made Lord Beaverbrook head of the Ministry for Aircraft Production (MAP), and he sought to increase production and reduce wasteful effort. Rather than tolerating the problematic Manchester, in late July 1940 Beaverbrook reduced the order to 200 and directed Avro to shift to producing the Halifax bomber instead. Yet after all these years of designing bombers that never flew, Chadwick was reluctant to yield the field to Handley Page, so in August he recommended substituting his four-engined Type 683 design, equipped with Rolls-Royce Merlin X engines, for the Manchester I. On 4 August Chadwick met with Beaverbrook and was able to convince him that he could complete the Type 683 prototype within six months, whereas switching to Halifax production would involve significant manufacturing problems.

Chadwick moved rapidly, lest the Air Ministry change its mind. In just four months he took a newly-built Manchester I and added ten more feet to the wings. With the airframe complete, he now had the problem of securing engines to power it. The Battle of Britain was raging, and Beaverbrook wanted all Rolls-Royce Merlin engines allocated for fighter production. When he refused to authorise four Merlins for Chadwick's new prototype, Avro was forced to surreptitiously acquire four Rolls-Royce Merlin Xs.

The design of the Lancaster revolved around its huge 33ft-long bomb-bay, which could carry 14 1,000lb bombs or larger weapons like the 4,000lb "cookie". In contrast, the Halifax had only a 22ft-long bomb-bay, and the Stirling could not carry any weapon larger than a 2,000lb bomb. The Lancaster's ability to carry large bombloads quickly made it the preferred aircraft of Bomber Command. (Imperial War Museum, CH 18554)

One of the early Lancaster B Is delivered to No. 44 "Rhodesia" Sqn conducts low-level flight training in April 1942. Although Lancasters normally flew above 10,000ft on operational sorties, they proved much less vulnerable to radar detection and German nightfighters when flown "on the deck". (Imperial War Museum, HU91969)

While the prototype was being completed in November, the Type 683 was designated as the Lancaster. Avro was able to complete the prototype before the Manchester I had even flown its first combat mission, and the aircraft made its first flight on January 9, 1941. Early test results were extremely promising thanks to the Lancaster's Rolls-Royce engines being both powerful and reliable, giving the aircraft double the range of the Manchester and a bomb load that was 35 per cent larger. Testing continued with the single prototype throughout the spring of 1941, which revealed that the Lancaster was also a significant improvement over both the Stirling and the Halifax. The troubled Manchester finally entered RAF service in February 1941, but recurrent mechanical failures resulted in the loss of more than 60 aircraft, and operational readiness rates were extremely poor.

Consequently, the Air Ministry decided to cut its losses and directed Avro to complete the last 43 Manchesters to the new four-engined Lancaster design. Although Chadwick had met his claim of building a flying Lancaster prototype within six months, Avro had great difficulty establishing the production line for these large bombers. Production output was only two aircraft per week beginning in October 1941, and it did not ramp up to ten per week until February 1942. Initially, it took A. V. Roe about 75,000 man hours to construct a single Lancaster, so in order to rapidly increase production, Lord Beaverbrook aligned multiple sub-contractors to assist the company – production times were significantly slashed by 1944. Bomber Command's No. 44 Sqn received the first production Lancasters on Christmas Eve 1941, and the unit immediately began converting crews to the new bomber. In RAF service, the Lancaster would soon prove to be a superb 'bomb truck', fully satisfying Churchill's and ACM Arthur Harris' desire to dump the largest tonnage of bombs on Germany as possible. However, the Lancaster was the result of a very flawed development process that glossed over technical and operational requirements in the name of expediency.

It is important to note that the Lancaster was initially designed as a general-purpose bomber, albeit with a heavy payload capacity, but with no real optimisation for the night-bombing role. By the time the Lancaster began operations in early 1942, Bomber Command relied upon night operations, and had gained first-hand experience of German nightfighter tactics. Yet even though the primary threat from nightfighters was almost certain to come from behind or below, two-thirds of the Lancaster's defensive armament was uselessly oriented towards the forward and upper arcs. No significant analysis about likely threats or lessons learned about nightfighting was incorporated into the Lancaster's design, and German nightfighters would soon learn to ruthlessly exploit its blind spot from below. The removal of the ventral turret that had been mounted on the Manchester and a few Lancaster B IIs in favour of the H2S radar installation was also made with little concern for the impact on bomber survivability.

Likewise, the continued use of 0.303in. machine guns for self-defence when Bf 110 *Nachtjäger* were already known to be using 20mm cannon was a particularly glaring design flaw in an otherwise well-built aircraft. Efforts to upgrade the Lancaster's armament were blocked by the Air Ministry until June 1943, when it reluctantly agreed to equip small numbers of Lancasters with 0.50in. heavy machine guns, either in FN 82 or Rose turrets. This improved defensive armament did not reach RAF squadrons until May 1944, and fewer than 400 bombers were upgraded.

Bf 110

Compared to the Lancaster, the development of the Bf 110 was fairly straightforward. Even before the official formation of the Luftwaffe, Oberstleutnant Wilhelm Wimmer in the C-Amt (Technical Department) of the RLM had drafted a series of requirements for German aviation companies to begin developing designs for combat aircraft. In June 1934 the RLM issued *Rüstungsflugzeug* IV (Armed Aircraft IV), a requirement for a two-seat heavy fighter with a speed of 400km/h, a range of 2,000km and 20mm cannon armament. The RLM staff conceived of this aircraft as a long-range bomber escort with an offensive role in mind, which was in line with the Luftwaffe's emphasis on bombers rather than fighters. Wimmer also envisioned the *Rüstungsflugzeug* IV as a multi-purpose aircraft, capable of performing reconnaissance and fighter-bomber missions.

After briefly considering proposals from six firms, the RLM awarded small development contracts to *Bayerische Flugzeugwerke* (BFW), Focke-Wulf and Henschel. None of these German companies had any real experience with designing multi-engined military aircraft, so the RLM was very cautious in moving forward on development, preferring to see tangible results before making a final decision on production. A further consideration was that while Germany had plenty of talented aviation designers, it had very few aircraft engines available to mount on new aircraft. This was due to the efforts of the Inter-Allied Commission of Control in restricting the development of new engines in Germany under the Treaty of Versailles. It was not until Hitler came to power in 1933 that the treaty was violated through the allocation of funds to the aviation industry. Nevertheless, there were only three German aircraft engine manufacturers in 1934 – Daimler-Benz, Junkers and BMW – who had limited manufacturing capacity and were still in the early stages of switching over from the development of commercial engines to a new generation of military powerplants.

BFW's chief designer, Willy Messerschmitt, was primarily involved in designing the Bf 109 prototype for the concurrent *Rüstungsflugzeug* III single-seat fighter competition, so the design work on the two-seat Bf 110 was led by Walter Rethel. Despite the daunting task of designing such an advanced military aircraft with limited experience and resources, Rethel's team was able to fabricate several mock-ups using Bf 109 components, while the RLM staff soon rejected the Focke-Wulf and Henschel prototypes as unsatisfactory. The main problem for Rethel was not fabrication of the fuselage but acquiring engines that could achieve the necessary high speed with an aircraft weighing more than seven tons when fully loaded.

Willy Messerschmitt designed the Bf 110 prototype in 1935-36 at the same time that he was developing the single-engined Bf 109. He left much of the work on the Bf 110 to his chief engineer Walter Rethel. Animosity between Erhard Milch, who headed the new German Air Ministry (RLM), and Messerschmitt threatened the awarding of the contract for the Bf 110 prototype, but the competing Focke-Wulf and Henschel designs proved unsatisfactory, so Messerschmitt won by default. (Author)

The unarmed Bf 110 V1 prototype made its first flight in May 1936. The Bf 110C production model entered Luftwaffe service in January 1939, and the aircraft remained a frontline combat type until April 1945. (Author)

Fitted with FuG 220 *Lichtenstein* SN-2 radar *Schräge Musik*, this Bf 110G-4 was assigned to the newly appointed *Gruppenkommandeur* of III./NJG 1, Oberleutnant Martin Drewes, in March 1944. His unit was based at Laon-Athies, in France, at the time. Note the 22 victory symbols and Knight's Cross painted on the fighter's fin. Having claimed two *Zerstörer* kills whilst serving with 4./ZG 76, Drewes became part of the *Nachtjagd* when his unit was redesignated 7./NJG 3 in November 1941. He enjoyed great success with this particular aircraft (fitted with both FuG 202 and FuG 22 *Lichtenstein* aerial intercept radar) after transferring to III./NJG 1 in March 1944, downing a total of five Lancasters that month, six in April and 14 in May – the fighter was destroyed in June 1944. Drewes managed to survive 235 missions in the *Nachtjagd*, and surrendered to the British in May 1945. By then he had scored a total of 52 victories, including at least 33 Lancasters.

By May 1936, Rethel's team had completed the Bf 110 V1 prototype, equipped with two Daimler-Benz DB 600A engines, capable of 910hp. On 12 May 1936 the unarmed Bf 110 V1 prototype made its first flight, which was rated a success. However, the development of combat-ready Bf 110s was delayed for another two years due to a shortage of Daimler-Benz engines, and instead the under-powered Junkers Jumo 210 engine was substituted on Bf 110A/B models that entered advanced Luftwaffe testing in 1937-38. It was not until January 1939 that the Luftwaffe received the Bf 110C fitted with improved DB 601A engines, which then served in the *Zerstörer* (destroyer) role as a daylight heavy fighter in the opening campaigns of World War II.

Since the development and early operations of the Bf 110C units are covered in *Osprey Duel 29 – Hurricane vs Bf 110*, it will not be repeated here. Yet while many accounts suggest that the Bf 110C was 'relegated' to nightfighter duty after its crippling losses in the Battle of Britain, it is important to note that NJG 1 was established and a Bf 110C achieved the *Nachtjagd's* first successful nocturnal interception a month before the *Zerstörer* units began suffering heavy losses in combat with RAF fighters. The Bf 110 had always been intended to engage enemy bombers, so the switch to a defensive role did not require any major modifications to the aircraft. However, the switch to a nightfighting role did. The early *Nachtjagd* units in 1940-41 were lash-up affairs, equipped with Bf 110Cs, Ds and Es that had only minor adjustments for nightfighting such as exhaust dampers to reduce their light signatures. Armament on these early *Nachtjagd* was essentially the same as carried by their daylight *Zerstörer* brethren, and the only on-board device they had to detect enemy bombers at night was the pilot's 'Mk I eyeball'.

However, Kammhuber was quick to realise that even if searchlights and radar could guide his Bf 110s to the general area of enemy bomber activity, his pilots still needed a means of detecting individual bombers in order to prosecute a successful interception. The German electrical firm AEG had been trying to perfect IR detection devices since 1935, and by 1941 it had made enough progress to provide Kammhuber's *Nachtjagd* with the *Spanner-Anlage Infrarot-Gerät*. The first version of *Spanner* was mounted on a Bf 110D-3, with an active IR searchlight fitted underneath the nose and a 'Q-Rohr' seeker mounted through the windscreen. The searchlight cast an infrared beam that reflected light from enemy bombers, which could then be viewed through the image intensifier seeker. The *Spanner* was put into limited operational use in mid-1941 on a few Bf 110s, but the detection range was only about 200m under the best conditions.

Bf 110G-4

42ft 9in.

13ft 8in.

53ft 4in.

G9 WD

Bf 110 pilots complained that by the time they found a target with *Spanner*, they could already see it with their own eyes! Nor was adding a bulky searchlight pod under the nose popular with Bf 110 aircrew. Experiments with IR gear continued, including a passive IR detector known as *Spanner II*, but neither Kammhuber nor his pilots regarded it as a solution to the on-board detection problem.

Contrary to popular mythology, it was the Germans who first developed the cavity magnetron that led to a breakthrough in radar development, not the British. Engineers at the firm GEMA GmbH had accomplished this feat in 1935, and the following year they managed to construct the *Freya* early warning radar.

Oberstleutnant Wolfgang Martini, in charge of the Oberkommando der Luftwaffe (OKL) communications department, worked closely with GEMA and became the biggest proponent of radar developments in the Luftwaffe. Martini succeeded in convincing the RLM to purchase 12 *Freya* sets in late 1936 and, after the Munich Crisis in 1938, to fund Telefunken's development of the *Würzburg* fire-control radar. Due to Martini's advocacy, the Luftwaffe purchased a number of these large, ground-based radars to assist their conventional flak units, which would later provide the essential ingredients for the Kammhuber Line in 1941.

However, it was not until April 1940 that Martini, now a Generalmajor, was able to convince Göring and the RLM of the need to develop a compact aerial intercept radar for use in aircraft. Telefunken was awarded a contract to develop this system, which would become the FuG 202 *Lichtenstein* B/C aerial radar. However, once the Luftwaffe realised that the Telefunken scientists wanted to mount a cluster of 32 dipole antennae on the nose of the fighter – which would increase drag and thereby decrease the aircraft's speed – the RLM ordered Telefunken to design the *Lichtenstein* with all equipment carried inside the aircraft. Although this was clearly impossible, Telefunken was forced to waste six months going down this futile path before the RLM finally relented and allowed them to mount the antennae where they belonged, on the nose of the aircraft. Once completed, the *Lichtenstein* B/C used a 75cm wavelength and had a range of about 2,000m.

After the Battle of Britain, the Luftwaffe fielded the Bf 110E in April 1941, with improved DB 601N engines. These radarless E-models belong to III./NJG 1, stationed at Rheine airfield, north of the Ruhr, in mid-1942. (Bundesarchiv, Bild 101I-360-2095-15, Foto: W. Wanderer)

By July 1941, Telefunken had a working prototype of the *Lichtenstein* B/C radar mounted on a Do 215 belonging to 4./NJG 1. On 9 August this aircraft shot down a Wellington bomber, demonstrating the effectiveness of the new radar. In an unusual display of sound judgment, Göring promoted Martini to *General der Luftnachrichtentruppe* and put him in charge of radar development for the Luftwaffe. Once empowered by Göring, Martini did something even more unusual in the Third Reich – he established a programme known as 'Rü Funk Aktion' to establish close ties between civilian scientists and *Nachtjagd* personnel in order to reduce the time-lag between technical developments reaching combat units and funnel 'lessons learned' type data back to Telefunken's technical teams. Once the FuG 202 *Lichtenstein* B/C radar demonstrated its effectiveness, Martini initiated Project *Adler* (Eagle) to equip the Bf 110E/U-1 nightfighters of I./NJG1 with the new radar. By the time that the Lancaster entered RAF service in quantity, the *Nachtjagd* would have a substantial number of radar-equipped Bf 110 nightfighters.

Yet just as Martini was solving the detection problem for the *Nachtjagd*, poor decisions made by the RLM were threatening to deprive them of aircraft upon which to mount the radars. Soon after the initial orders for the Bf 110C were placed in 1938, the RLM directed Willy Messerschmitt to begin designing an improved, follow-on heavy fighter to replace the Bf 110. Within a year, Messerschmitt's team had a flying prototype, designated the Me 210, which seemed to represent a vast improvement over the Bf 110. However, the new design was inherently unstable, and its lengthy development became a fiasco for the Luftwaffe's *Nachtjagd*. Believing that Messerschmitt would soon resolve the Me 210's difficulties, the RLM assigned very low priority to Bf 110 production after the Battle of Britain. The Bf 110E and F models were only introduced in early 1941 as slightly improved versions of the C-model, and production dropped off sharply after August 1941 as the Me 210 began entering service. Then just as Martini was getting ready to deploy the *Lichtenstein* B/C radar, the RLM arbitrarily decided to terminate all Bf 110 production. Soon afterwards the Me 210 programme began to completely unravel as early production models

A Bf 110G-4 nightfighter with four large FuG 220B *Lichtenstein* SN-2b radar antennae surrounding one smaller FuG 212 *Lichtenstein* C-1 antenna. Many Bf 110 pilots disliked the additional weight caused by large nose-mounted antenna arrays, which cost them about 40mph in speed. Note that this aircraft also has additional 20mm cannon fitted in a centreline belly pack. (Author)

proved to be unsatisfactory. Lacking any other flyable alternatives, the RLM was forced to put the Bf 110F back in production in February 1942, while requesting that Messerschmitt develop an improved Bf 110G model to mount even better radar and weapons in 1943.

Even after reinstating Bf 110 production, deliveries were limited to only 50-60 aircraft of all models per month, which dragged out the re-equipping of the *Nachtjagd* throughout 1942-43. It is important to note that a sizeable portion of Bf 110 production continued to go towards ground attack and reconnaissance models; nightfighter versions did not receive priority until June 1944.

Several pre-production G-models were ready by June 1942, but the *Nachtjagd* did not receive any for squadron service until February 1943. After mid-1943, the *Nachtjagd* would focus primarily on keeping the various versions of the Bf 110G-4 nightfighter as technically up-to-date as possible and built in reasonable quantity. Following the demise of the Me 210 programme, the Luftwaffe leadership hoped that the He 219 nightfighter would be a viable substitute when it entered service in June 1943, but Heinkel was never able to build this impressive aircraft in the quantities needed to re-equip more than a handful of *Nachtjagd* squadrons.

In seeking to keep an essentially obsolescent aircraft like the Bf 110 available for frontline service well after its prime, the *Nachtjagd* leadership was unusually receptive to novel ideas. Since 1941, some German pilots had been experimenting with mounting upward-firing weapons in their aircraft, and by 1942 they had official sanction from Kammhuber to begin technical tests.

Hauptmann Rudolf Schönert, commander of II./NJG 5, was one of the most ardent proponents of upward-firing guns. Indeed, he mounted four 20mm MG 151 cannon in a Do 217N that he used to shoot down a Lancaster in April 1943. The new tactic was nicknamed *Schräge Musik*, and it enabled German nightfighters equipped with such weaponry to attack Lancaster bombers from below with little or no warning. The cannons were usually mounted in the rear of the cockpit at a 70-degree angle and the 20mm cannon were equipped with flash suppressors and either dimmed tracers or none at all, so that the bomber crews could not detect where the firing was coming from. Select Bf 110 crews began to receive *Schräge Musik* kits in the summer of 1943, and they were first used in combat in August of that year. When the tactic proved successful, the *Nachtjagd* began mounting the weaponry on more fighters until about one-fifth of Bf 110s were equipped with it by mid-1944. Despite its obsolescent design, the Bf 110 would remain in production until February 1945, and it fought on until war's end.

TECHNICAL SPECIFICATIONS

Bf 110

Bf 110C

This version of the Bf 110 was the first large-scale production model of the *Zerstörer*. It appeared in early 1939 and remained in production until the spring of 1941. The *Nachtjagd* was initially equipped with the Bf 110C-4 in 1940, but its numbers dwindled to only 30-35 aircraft by early 1942. Thereafter, small numbers of C-models

Bf 110C wk-nr 3920 was assigned to the first *Geschwaderkommodore* of NJG 1, Major Wolfgang Falck. Painted black overall, and bearing the unit emblem on its nose, the aircraft has its engines run up at Arnhem, in Holland, in the autumn of 1940. (via Jerry Scutts)

remained operational until October-December 1943. The Bf 110C-4 was fitted with two 1,050hp DB 601A engines, which gave it a maximum speed of 349mph and a typical mission endurance of just over two hours. Armament consisted of two 20mm MG FF cannons and four 7.92mm MG 17 machine guns mounted in the nose, and one rearward-firing 7.92mm MG 15 machine gun for the radio operator. Since few of these models received radar, most only had a two-man crew.

Bf 110D

The D-model was an extended-range version of the Bf 110C, and it first appeared in May 1940. Remaining in *Nachtjagd* service until December 1943, the most common variant in use as a nightfighter was the Bf 110D-3, of which 253 were built. The Bf 110D was slower and less manoeuvrable than the C-model due to its extra fuel tanks, but it had a mission endurance of three hours. Experiments with mounting the *Spanner Anlage* active infrared searchlight and 'Q-Rohr' seeker were conducted on Bf 110D-3s in an early, but unsuccessful, effort to improve the aircraft's night-detection capabilities.

Bf 110E

The Bf 110E entered service from April 1941, and the E-1 and E-2 variants remained in frontline use with *Nachtjagd* units until December 1943. A total of 655 Bf 110E-1s and E-2s were built. The E-model was primarily intended to improve the base performance of the aircraft by equipping it with two 1,250hp DB 601N engines, which increased its maximum speed to 311mph. This model also continued the shift towards a dedicated nightfighter, with a third crew position being added. The Bf 110E/U1 model was the first equipped with the FuG 202 *Lichtenstein* B/C radar in March 1942.

Bf 110F-4

The first Bf 110 variant built specifically for the *Nachtjagd* role, the F-4 served from December 1941 to August 1944. A total of 283 F-4s were built by the Gotha Waggonfabrik (GWF). It was equipped with two 1,350hp DB 601F engines, providing it with a maximum speed of 352mph. Through the use of small drop tanks, the F-4 had a mission endurance of 2.5 hours. The F-model was designed to carry the FuG 202 *Lichtenstein* aerial intercept radar, although this did not become standard equipment until mid-1942. In an effort to protect the crew from bombers' 0.303in. return fire, 57mm thick bullet-resistant glass was installed in front of the pilot's windscreen. The Bf 110F-4/U1 was the first variant to mount two upward-firing 20mm MG FF cannon in the *Schräge Musik* configuration in the rear of the canopy.

A Bf 110E of II./NJG 1 is refuelled in the summer of 1942. The fighter was built around its heavy nose-mounted armament of two 20mm cannon and four 7.92mm machine guns, which could tear a bomber's fuselage apart with a two-second burst. The Lancaster remained hopelessly outgunned by the Bf 110 for the duration. (Bundesarchiv, Bild 101I-359-2048-12A, Foto: Doelfs)

Bf 110G-4

The G-4 was the definitive nightfighter model of the Bf 110. Although six pre-production examples were built in June 1942, series production did not begin for a further six months due to delays with the variant's new engines. Indeed, the Bf 110G-4 did not enter *Nachtjagd* service until February 1943. It remained in production until February 1945 and in operational use until war's end. A total of 2,191 G-4s were built by GWF and the Luther-Werke Braunschweig (LWB). Despite the upgrade to two 1,475hp DB 605B engines, the addition of radar antenna arrays and other equipment limited the aircraft's maximum speed to 317mph, which was barely 30mph faster than the Lancaster. The Bf 110G-4 had a mission endurance of three hours.

A Bf 110F-4 of 4./NJG 1 undergoes servicing on the ramp at St Trond airfield, in Belgium, during the summer of 1942. This aircraft has been fitted with FuG 202 *Lichtenstein* aerial intercept radar, the system's antenna array clearly visible forward of the nose. The "N" on the engine cowling denotes that the fighter is powered by a pair of DB 601Ns. (via Jerry Scutts)

The armament installed in the G-4 varied considerably from unit to unit, but the weaponry fitted in the nose often included either two 30mm Mk 108 or two 20mm MG 151 cannons and four MG 17 machine guns. Twenty per cent of Bf 110G-4s were equipped with the R-8 field kit for *Schräge Musik*, which usually consisted of two 20mm MG FF cannons. The Bf 110G-4 carried a wide variety of aerial intercept radars during 1943-45, including the FuG 212, 220 and 227. Some G-4 models were fitted with up-armoured 90mm thick windscreens.

By early 1944 the Bf 110G-4 had become the primary nightfighter in 15 *Nachtjagd gruppen* and virtually all the older models of the aircraft had been transferred to training units. During the last two years of the war the *Nachtjagd* employed multiple variants, and modifications, of the Bf 110G in service, tailored to mission requirements.

A group of Bf 110G-4 nightfighters from NJG 4, possibly at Florennes airfield, in Belgium, in mid-1944. The introduction of the improved FuG 220 *Lichtenstein* SN-2 radar in 1943 swung the duel back in favour of the Luftwaffe for a while. (Bundesarchiv, Bild 101I-492-3347-028, Foto: Güntzel)

BF 110G-4 ARMAMENT

The Bf 110G-4 was built to provide a stable platform for its cannons, supplemented by quad machine guns, to defeat enemy bombers at close range. The standard twin 20mm Mauser MG 151/20 cannons and four 7.92mm Rheinmetall MG 17 machine guns in the nose were retained from the earlier Bf 110C configuration, although the upward-firing *Schräge Musik* 20mm Oerlikon MG FF cannon did not appear until the Bf 110F-4 model in 1942. The Bf 110G-4's armament provided it with the firepower to attack and quickly defeat the Lancaster either with a standard rear attack (*von unten hinten*) or from below with *Schräge Musik*, to exploit the blind spot beneath the bomber. When using *Schräge Musik*, the Bf 110G-4 could attack the Lancaster with near impunity.

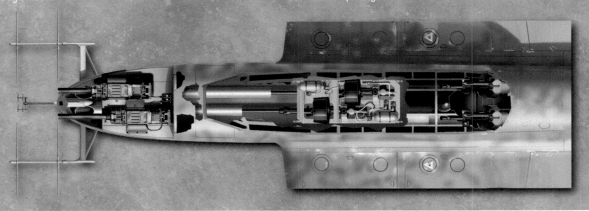

LANCASTER

Bomber Command used four primary models of Lancaster in the strategic bombing campaign against Germany in 1942-45. Unlike the Bf 110, Lancaster production was totally allocated towards a single mission, and role.

LANCASTER I

A No. 44 "Rhodesia" Sqn Lancaster on the ground at Waddington, in Lincolnshire, in 1942. While the Lancaster represented a very aerodynamically "clean" design that pleased its crews with its flying performance, to *Nachtjagd* crews it was very vulnerable from behind due to its poor rearward situational awareness and defensive firepower. (Imperial War Museum, TR 192)

No fewer than 3,425 Lancaster Is were built between November 1941 and March 1946. This version was initially powered by four 1,460hp Rolls-Royce Merlin XX engines, which were later upgraded to Merlin 22s or 24s. Fully loaded with 12,000lb of bombs, the Mk I had a maximum speed of 275mph and a ceiling of 24,500ft. With a typical cruising speed of 239mph, the Mk I had an operational range that varied between 1,730 and 2,530 miles, depending upon bomb load. For defensive armament, the Lancaster I was equipped with Frazer-Nash hydraulically powered nose, dorsal and tail turrets, for a total of ten 0.303in. machine guns. The FN 20 rear

RAF mechanics conduct maintenance on a Lancaster's port outer Rolls-Royce Merlin engine. The Merlin was a superb powerplant, and it provided the Lancaster with the ability to carry very large bomb loads. Bf 110 pilots equipped with *Schräge Musik* upward-firing cannon usually aimed here, between the two engines on the port wing, so as to ignite the Lancaster's fuel tanks. (Imperial War Museum, TR 20)

Lancasters under construction in mid-1943. The V-shaped antenna below the rear gun turret is the ARRI 5664 *Monica* Mk I tail-warning device. Not only did *Monica* fail to alert the Lancaster crews about approaching nightfighters, but the Germans quickly found out about it from downed wreckage and created the *Flensburg* device to home in on *Monica* emissions. The introduction of *Monica* actually helped the Bf 110s to find and destroy more Lancasters. (Imperial War Museum, TR1384)

turret provided the main defence against nightfighters, with four 0.303in. machine guns that could traverse about 80 degrees to either port or starboard and depress down to -45 degrees. The Lancaster carried 9,792 litres of fuel, split evenly between three tanks in each wing.

LANCASTER II

Due to a shortage of Merlin engines, the Mk II was developed with four 1,735hp Bristol Hercules VI or XVI engines as substitutes. As it turned out, the Merlin shortage was illusory and only 301 Mk IIs were built between September 1942 and March 1944. This model had a slight reduction in weight, but its overall performance was essentially unchanged. The Mk II also had larger bomb-bays to accommodate the RAF's new generation of 8,000lb bombs. Perhaps the most significant difference between the Mk II and the Mk I was the addition of a ventral turret with two additional 0.303in. machine guns, which offered some protection against attacks from below. The Lancaster Mk IIs were assigned to four Canadian and two British bomber squadrons.

LANCASTER III

3,039 Mk IIIs were built between November 1942 and June 1945, this variant being powered by Packard-built 1,460hp Merlin 28 and 38 engines.

LANCASTER X

Constructed in Ontario, Canada, some 430 Mk Xs were produced between September 1943 and May 1945. The Mk X was equipped with Packard-built 1,460hp Rolls-Royce Merlin 224 engines.

Bf 110G-4 and Lancaster B III Comparison Specifications		
	Bf 110G-4	**Lancaster B III**
Powerplant	2 x 1,475hp DB 605B	4 x 1,460hp Merlin 28
Dimensions		
Span	53ft 4in.	102ft 0in.
Length	42ft 9in.	69ft 6in.
Height	13ft 8in.	20ft 6in.
Wing Area	413 sq ft	1,300 sq ft
Weights		
Empty	11,200lb	39,600lb
Loaded	17,158lb	65,000lb
Performance		
Max Speed	343mph	272mph
Range	656 miles (with tanks)	875 miles
Service Ceiling	36,000ft	24,500ft
Armament	2 x 20mm MG 151/20 5 x 7.92mm MG 17 2 x 20mm MG FF	8 x 0.303in. Brownings

ANALYTIC FACTORS

FIREPOWER

If a Bf 110 could detect and close with a Lancaster at night, its armament gave it an enormous advantage. The nightfighter's firepower was based upon 20mm cannons, the twin Mauser MG 151/20 weapons in the lower nose of the Bf 110 being capable of pumping 1,500 armour-piercing or high explosive (HE) rounds per minute into the rear of a Lancaster. The cannons were augmented by four 7.92mm Rheinmetall MG 17 machine guns that could fire 4,800 rpm from their location in the fighter's upper nose. German statistical analysis of *Nachtjagd* combat indicated that a Lancaster could be shot down with just 18-20 hits from a 20mm cannon, equivalent to a two-second burst. A particularly deadly advantage was provided by the 20mm *Minen-Geschoß* HE-M round, which had three times the blast effect of a standard HE round. Such ordnance could tear apart the structure of a Lancaster bomber.

In contrast, the Lancaster's defensive firepower was fatally compromised by the fact that only the rear turret could really contribute to protecting the aircraft against dead astern attacks and the quad 0.303in. machine guns in the FN 20 turret were no match for two MG 151/20 cannons and four MG 17s. Even at typical night engagement ranges of 100-300m, it was extremely difficult for Lancaster rear turret gunners to detect, engage and hit a Bf 110. British tests on the ground indicated that two-thirds of all 0.303in. bullets that hit an aircraft fuselage at a range of 180m were deflected, and only six per cent penetrated even 4mm of armour plate. When *Schräge Musik* was added into the equation, the inability of the Lancaster's defensive armament to engage targets directly below the bomber was a fatal weakness.

MANOEUVRABILITY

The earlier versions of the Bf 110, such as the F-4, had a considerable speed advantage over Lancasters, allowing for rapid approaches or a breakaway as needed. However, once the *Lichtenstein* radar and heavier armament was added, the later marks of Bf 110 lost their decisive edge in speed and power-to-weight ratio over the Lancaster. The additional weight added to the Bf 110G-4 also increased its wing loading to 243kg/m^3, which was similar to the Lancaster's wing load of 240kg/m^3. The standard Lancaster defensive tactic when it detected an approaching Bf 110 was to initiate a corkscrew manoeuvre that involved a rapid dive that could increase speed to about 300mph, followed by a sudden climb, then another dive, until the nightfighter was shaken off the tail. For many novice or average Bf 110 pilots, the corkscrew was enough to ruin their approach, and they would often break off the attack. However, against experienced Bf 110 pilots the corkscrew often did not work. Overall, the Bf 110 had just enough of a speed advantage to catch a Lancaster, but with little margin to spare.

A Lancaster from No. 550 Sqn that limped home after being shot up by a Bf 110 over Berlin on the night of 30/31 January 1944. The nightfighter pilot had used the standard *'von unten hinten'* tactic to kill both the rear turret and mid-upper turret gunners. Note the large holes in the tail unit and fuselage, possibly from 20mm *Minen-Geschoß* hits. (Imperial War Museum, CE 121)

HIDE AND SEEK

In 1941, the nightfighter's ability to detect the bomber, and vice versa, was roughly equal, and dependent upon available illumination and alert crewmen. However, once the Germans developed the *Himmelbett* system and deployed *Lichtenstein* radars in Bf 110 nightfighters, the advantage shifted markedly in favour of the Germans and Lancaster losses rose sharply. Through the employment of *Window* and sophisticated jamming techniques, Bomber Command was able to temporarily erase the German advantage in mid-1943 and reduce its losses, but the Luftwaffe later recovered with improved radars and anti-jamming tactics. In this factor, neither side enjoyed a permanent advantage in the aerial duel, only periods of greater or lesser success.

MISSION ENDURANCE

Although developed as a long-range heavy fighter, the Bf 110F/G models still had a maximum mission endurance of only three hours. Given time spent waiting on station for vectoring instructions, it was not uncommon for Bf 110 crews to run out of fuel before targets entered their sector. It was thus imperative that Luftwaffe *jagddivision* commanders chose the right time to scramble their fighters, lest they run low on fuel before the battle proper had begun. In this factor, the Lancaster had a clear advantage over the Bf 110, and with its 12-hour mission endurance it could afford to employ tactics such as low flying to avoid enemy nightfighters.

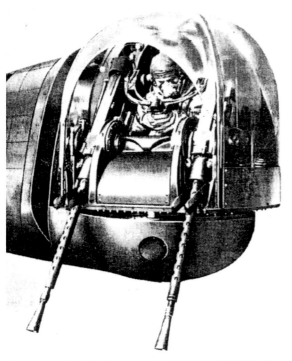

EXTERNAL COMMUNICATIONS

Unlike the Lancaster, which was designed as a self-sufficient fighting unit (although later aided by radio navigation devices), the Bf 110 could not function effectively as a nightfighter without radio communications with its ground controllers. The Bf 110 maintained contact with its fighter control centre via the FuG 10 high-frequency radio, which could receive or transmit both voice and Morse code signals. Once the RAF developed aerial jammers, like the Lancaster ABC, the vulnerability of the Bf 110's radio communications link seriously undermined its ability to find targets or even navigate at night over German airspace. External communications proved to be the primary Achilles heel of the Bf 110 nightfighter.

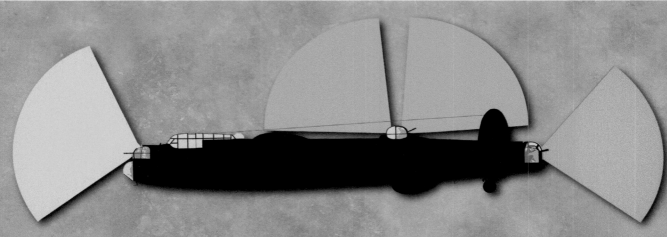

LANCASTER FIELDS-OF-FIRE

The standard Lancaster B I and B III were equipped with ten 0.303in. (7.7mm) machine guns mounted in three powered turrets, which covered the frontal (FN 5A), rear (FN 20) and upper (FN 50) arcs fairly well, but which left a large undefended gap beneath the bomber – German nightfighters learned to exploit this. Both the original Manchester and the Lancaster B II were equipped with a ventral turret to provide protection underneath the bomber, but B II production represented only four per cent of all Lancasters built. The Air Ministry had recognised the inadequacy of the 0.303in. machine gun to defeat German fighters as early as 1938, but Bomber Command made no serious effort to provide the Lancaster with the more lethal 0.50in. machine gun until May 1944, and then only 180 aircraft received the upgraded FN 82 turret and another 227 the Rose turret.

PROTECTION

German data indicates that the Lancaster required about 20 per cent less damage than the B-17 Flying Fortress to shoot it down. Against *Schräge Musik*, which aimed at the fuel tanks in the wings, the Lancaster was extremely vulnerable as it was prone to bursting into flames. Due to a narrow escape hatch, the Lancaster also proved to be a death trap for its crew if the aircraft was set on fire by German nightfighters. While the Stirling and Halifax both had a 25 per cent crew survival rate, the Lancaster had only a 15 per cent survival rate. In contrast, the Bf 110G-4 was provided with an armoured windscreen that could deflect 0.303in. bullets, and the only vulnerability was hits on either engine. If forced to abandon their aircraft, Bf 110 crews had about a 50 per cent probability of survival. Indeed, many aircrew lost at least one aircraft during their frontline careers.

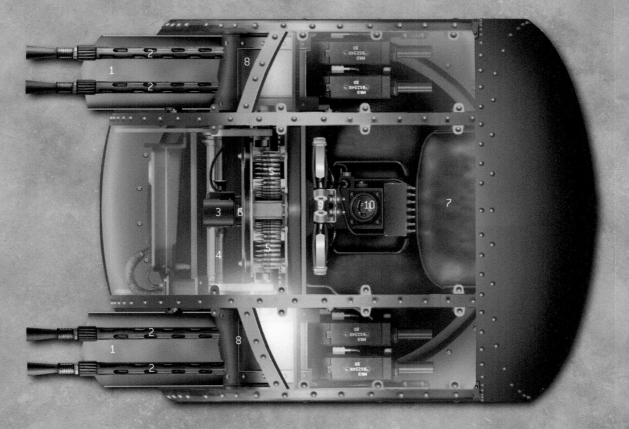

LANCASTER B I FN 20 REAR TURRET

1. Cartridge ejection chutes
2. Browning 0.303in. machine guns
3. Barr & Stroud Mk III reflector gunsight
4. Gunsight mounting arm
5. 0.303in. ammunition belts
6. Ammunition feed sprockets and feed guides
7. Gunner's seat
8. Swivelling gun chassis
9. Turret control yoke, handgrips and firing buttons
10. Oxygen gauge

THE STRATEGIC SITUATION

'From this [calculations] it appears that the Lancaster force alone should be sufficient, but only just sufficient, to produce in Germany by 1 April 1944 a state of devastation in which surrender is inevitable.'
ACM Harris in a letter to Prime Minister Winston Churchill, 3 November 1943

'Everything must be staked on the [Bf] 110. Only the 110 in sufficient numbers can give us the necessary relief at night.'
Generalfeldmarschall Erhard Milch

In early 1942 the Lancaster reached an initial operational capability within Bomber Command just as major changes were re-shaping the RAF's strategic bombing campaign. The first stage of Britain's bomber offensive over Germany, from May 1940 to February 1942, had been conducted in such an amateurish and incoherent manner that it had failed to inflict significant economic or psychological damage upon the Third Reich. Although Bomber Command had caused some damage to the Ruhr industrial cities, the pre-war twin-engined bombers lacked the range and payload to reach Berlin or other targets deep in Germany. Furthermore, Bomber Command's efforts to conduct precision night bombing had been revealed by the Butt Report in August 1941 to be a failure, with at best only 10-20 per cent of bombers striking within five miles of their intended target. What good would Lancasters be to Britain's war effort if they couldn't reliably hit critical enemy targets? Put on the defensive by this excoriating statistical analysis, Bomber Command sought a new rationale, based on what its forces could actually achieve.

On 14 February 1942, the Air Ministry issued General Directive No. 5, known as the Area Bombing Directive, which directed Bomber Command to concentrate its operations against Germany's major cities in order to degrade civilian morale within the Third Reich. In practical terms, this now meant that the achievements of Bomber Command's growing fleet of four-engined heavy bombers would be measured primarily by the gross bomb tonnage delivered to Germany, as if it were some great assembly line, rather than by inflicting crippling damage on specific targets that were vital to the Third Reich's war machine. On 22 February, Bomber Command also received a new commander, ACM Arthur Harris, who had played a role in developing the requirements for the Lancaster and was enthusiastic about its capabilities – he referred to it as 'that shining sword'. Harris also had an almost religious faith in area bombing and its ability to defeat Germany, and intended to remove the doubt cast upon Bomber Command by the Butt Report.

When No. 44 'Rhodesia' Sqn became the first combat-ready Lancaster unit in March 1942, Bomber Command had almost 600 frontline bombers (not including aircraft in conversion and training units), but two-thirds of them were still twin-engined types and fewer than 200 were four-engined Stirlings, Halifaxes and Lancasters. Avro's production of the Lancaster in the first half of 1942 was limited to 30-50 aircraft per month, which was just sufficient to convert one twin-engined bomber squadron per month. The Lancaster made its first appearance over Germany's skies on the night of 10/11 March 1942, when exactly two Lancasters participated in a raid with 124 other aircraft on Essen. Harris was very impressed with the Lancaster from the beginning, particularly its range and bomb-load, which exceeded that of the Halifax. Believing that the Lancaster was a 'super weapon', on 17 April Harris ordered the two available Lancaster squadrons to mount a long-range daylight raid on Augsburg, in southern Bavaria. Harris' willingness to disregard German defences cost both Lancaster squadrons dearly, with seven of twelve participating aircraft being shot down by flak and Luftwaffe day fighters.

The idiotic and suicidal Augsburg raid prematurely disclosed the new heavy bomber's capabilities to the Luftwaffe before it was available to the RAF in quantity. Despite these catastrophic losses, Harris continued to dabble with employing Lancasters in low-level daylight penetration raids throughout the remainder of the war, even as he used it to spearhead his night bomber offensive over the Third Reich's cities. By June 1942 Harris had eight squadrons with 128 Lancasters, all in No. 5 Group.

A Lancaster from No. 3 Group's No. 75 "New Zealand" Sqn is loaded with bombs at Mepal, in Cambridgeshire, prior to participating in a night raid over Germany. By 1944, Bomber Command was aware that between ten and 30 per cent of the bombs it was dropping were failing to explode due to faulty fuses. A number of Lancasters were also destroyed by their own bombs detonating prematurely. (Imperial War Museum CH 14680)

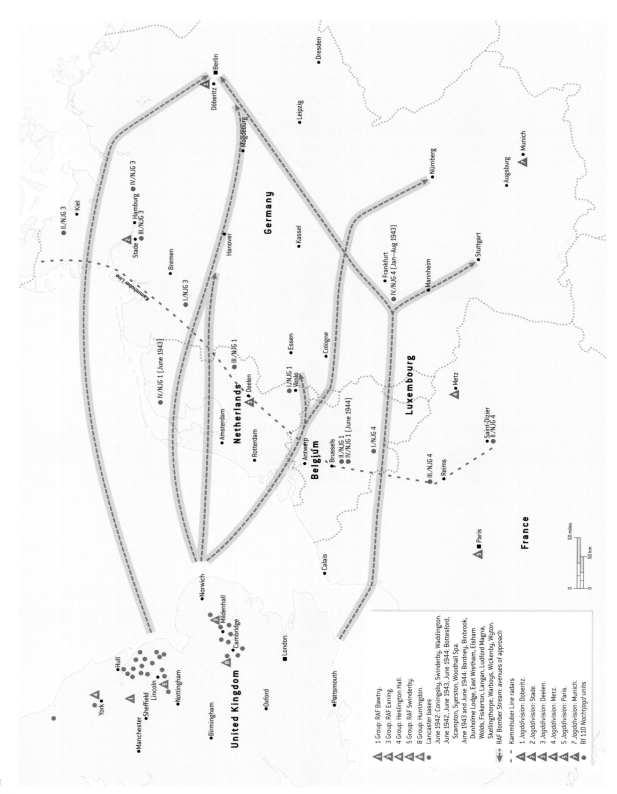

Kiel
● II/NJG 3

Dresden ●

Berlin ■
Döberitz ●

Leipzig ●

Germany

Magdeburg

Hamburg ●
Stade ● ● III/NJG 3
IV/NJG 3

Bremen ●

Hanover ●

Kassel ●

Nürnberg ●

Münich ●
Augsburg ●

Kammhuber Line

I/NJG 3 ●

Frankfurt ●
IV/NJG 4 [Jan–Aug 1943]

Mannheim ●

Stuttgart ■

IV/NJG 1 [June 1943]

Essen ●
Cologne ●

III/NJG 1 ●

Amsterdam ●
Deelen ●

Venlo ●
I/NJG 1 ●

Netherlands

Rotterdam ●

Luxembourg

Metz ▲

Saint-Dizier
II/NJG 4 ●

Antwerp ●
Brussels ●
I/NJG 1 ●
IV/NJG 1 [June 1944] ●
I/NJG 4 ●

Belgium

III/NJG 4 ●
Reims ●

Calais ●

Paris ■

France

50 miles
0
0   50 km

Hull ●
York ▲

Manchester ●
Sheffield ●
Lincoln ●
Nottingham ●

Birmingham ●

Norwich ●
Mildenhall ●
Cambridge ●

Oxford ●

London ■

Portsmouth ●

United Kingdom

1 Group: RAF Bawtry.
3 Group: RAF Exning.
4 Group: Heslington Hall.
5 Group: RAF Swinderby.
8 Group: Huntingdon.
Lancaster bases
June 1942: Coningsby, Swinderby, Waddington.
June 1942, June 1943, June 1944: Bottesford,
  Scampton, Syerston, Woodhall Spa.
June 1943 and June 1944: Bardney, Binbrook,
  Dunholme Lodge, East Wretham, Elsham
  Wolds, Fiskerton, Langan, Ludford Magna,
  Skellingthorpe, Warboys, Wickenby, Wyton.
RAF Bomber Stream: avenues of approach

Kammhuber Line radars
1 Jagddivision: Döberitz.
2 Jagddivision: Stade.
3 Jagddivision: Deelen.
4 Jagddivision: Metz.
5 Jagddivision: Paris.
7 Jagddivision: Munich.
Bf 110 Nachtjagd units

The duel between Lancasters and Bf 110s would be shaped by three strategic trends that began to surface in 1942. First, Bomber Command under Harris would dramatically increase the scale and ferocity of strategic bombing over Germany. The OBOE (Objective Bombing of Enemy) blind-bombing system had been introduced in December 1941 and the GEE radio navigation system was ready for mass use by March 1942. With improved navigation and bomb accuracy, Bomber Command could finally fulfil its objectives of smashing German cities. Whereas raids in 1941 had generally involved between 80-160 bombers and inflicted only a few dozen casualties on German cities, Harris would quickly escalate to raids involving hundreds of bombers that could inflict thousands of casualties. He and other RAF leaders also began advocating a '4,000-bomber' force, which they argued could defeat Germany. Harris and other leaders in the Air Ministry regarded the Lancaster as a war-winning weapon, and they were able to convince Churchill to allocate substantial resources towards its production. Thanks to the flow of American Lend Lease aid, Churchill could afford to concentrate Britain's industries on heavy bomber construction, instead of on tanks, artillery, landing craft or merchant ships. Consequently, Britain's output of heavy bombers increased dramatically in 1943-44, enabling Harris to field much larger forces than his predecessors.

During 1941-45, the MAP spent about £236 million acquiring 7,377 Lancaster bombers, making the aircraft's production one of the most expensive British weapons programmes of World War II. The Lancaster bomber force also required exorbitant logistical support, including a large share of Britain's limited supply of 100-octane fuel. In order to reach Berlin with a full bomb load, a single Lancaster required 2,075 gallons (9.5 tons) of 100-octane fuel, almost all of which had to be imported from the United States, Azerbaijan or Trinidad through U-boat-infested waters.

	Bf 110 production		Lancaster production	
	Annual	Monthly	Annual	Monthly
1941	786	65	10	3
1942	581	48	688	57
1943	1,509	125	1,981	161
1944	1,518	126	3,046	253
1945	110	40	1,648	137

The second strategic factor that shaped the Lancaster versus Bf 110 duel was the increasing lethality of the German *Nachtjagd* force. Kammhuber finally established a series of contiguous air defence zones known as *Himmelbett* from Denmark to northern France by the end of 1941, and by spring 1942 he had nine *gruppen* with 150 Bf 110 (mostly D- and E-models) and 35 Do 215/217 nightfighters deployed in northwest Europe. The Luftwaffe's *Funkhorchdienst* (signal intercept service) had become adept at detecting Bomber Command's habit of tuning their aircraft radios just before a raid, which was then disseminated to individual *Nachtjagd* units to place them on alert. Once a raid was airborne, nightfighters would scramble and orbit, one in each *Himmelbett* zone. Each zone was centred upon a 1.2m wavelength *Freya* early

warning radar, which had a range of 200km. When the radar detected a target, range and bearing information was relayed to the fighter by a *Jägerleitoffizier* (Fighter Control Officer [JLO]) via high-frequency (HF) radio. The Bf 110 crew would then head towards the target and either acquire it visually or, if they were lucky enough to have a FuG 202 *Lichtenstein* AI radar, pick it up at a range of two kilometres. By early 1942 the Luftwaffe had perfected the *Himmelbett* system and learned to coordinate its ground-based radars with its nightfighters. The *Nachtjagd* now had a trained cadre of Bf 110 aircrew who were adept at using Ground Control Intercept (GCI) tactics and who began steadily racking up kills in their designated *Himmelbett* zones. Bomber Command losses nearly doubled in 1942 as the improved *Nachtjagd* force

In 1941 the Luftwaffe deployed a belt of *Freya* (right) and *Würzburg* (left) early warning radars stretching from Denmark to northern France to detect incoming British bombers. Under the *Himmelbett* system, the Bf 110 nightfighters were initially tied to operating in specific radar zones. (Bundesarchiv, Bild 141-2732)

brought its skills to bear. However, Kammhuber's system was essentially a static defence, and vulnerable if its Command and Control (C2) was disrupted. Furthermore, Hitler refused to devote significant resources to reinforce the *Nachtjagd*, since he was firmly focused on the war in the East.

The third strategic factor that shaped the duel between the Lancaster and Bf 110 was the growing importance of electronic detection and electronic countermeasures. The Luftwaffe gained an initial advantage in the use of radar to direct its Bf 110 nightfighters, which deprived Bomber Command of its main advantage – the relative invisibility of night operations. In response, the RAF leadership turned to the Countermeasures Group of the Telecommunications Research Establishment (TRE), established in Dorset in May 1940. British scientists had limited knowledge of the frequencies used by Luftwaffe radars until the commando raid on Bruneval in February 1942 secured parts of a *Würzburg* radar. Analysis of this radar led to the development of aluminium strips that were cut to the correct length to provide false returns on German radar sets. Harris knew about this countermeasure, which was designated *Window*, but wanted to pick his moment to use it. The TRE also helped Bomber Command to develop means to

The Luftwaffe's deployment of the Telefunken-designed FuG 202 B/C *Lichtenstein* airborne intercept radar in NJG 1's Bf 110F-4 fighters based in Holland from February 1942 was a game-changer. The improvement of the Bf 110's ability to hunt targets in the dark came just as the Lancaster was joining the air campaign over Germany. (Author)

jam Luftwaffe communications, as well as defensive equipment such as *Monica* and the FN 121 AGLT. On the other side, Telefunken and Siemens sought to counter British electronic advances by developing the improved FuG 220 SN-radar for the Bf 110, as well as a host of passive radar detectors such as *Flensburg*, *Neptun* and *Naxos*. Both sides' scientists were quick to take advantage of captured enemy electronic equipment, which often led to short-term benefits. Indeed, the contest between scientists on either side was a key part of the Lancaster versus Bf 110 duel.

Operational factors and evolving doctrine on both sides also shaped the Lancaster versus Bf 110 duel. By 1942, Bomber Command recognised that a Lancaster could pass through a *Himmelbett* grid in less than four minutes, which meant that the bomber was only at risk from nightfighters for a brief part of its mission. *Himmelbett* was essentially a static zone defence, and even though Bomber Command could not easily bypass it, the grid system could be overwhelmed. Each *Freya* radar could only prosecute one interception at a time, which was adequate when Bomber Command obliged by sending its bombers through an area a few at a time. Furthermore, German ground controllers could only handle one Bf 110 per *Himmelbett* zone, which prevented the *Nachtjagd* from massing its forces. Harris changed the operational and tactical dynamic by introducing a dense bomber stream in May 1942, which channelled all the bombers through a few boxes and packed them into a much tighter formation, thereby overwhelming the handful of fighters in their path with too many targets. It is important to note that the introduction of GEE, which enabled improved

Once the British learned that German early warning radars operated on only four frequencies, their scientists were able to develop aluminium chaff strips known as *Window* to confuse enemy radars. Here, Lancasters drop clouds of *Window* over the Ruhr. The introduction of *Window* switched the advantage to Bomber Command, and for a time Lancaster losses declined. (Imperial War Museum, C5635)

In this still taken from a ciné film shot by a No. 463 Sqn Lancaster, two more Lancasters can be seen surrounded by flak bursts over Pforzheim, Germany, on the night of 23/24 February 1945. This attack proved to be the third most destructive Bomber Command raid of the war, with a firestorm killing 17,600 people in the city. However, Bf 110s from NJG 6 were still in the fight, and they shot down the raid's Master Bomber (South African Flt Lt Erwin Swales of No. 582 Sqn in Lancaster PB538) and 14 other Lancasters. (Imperial War Museum, C 5007)

After the RAF's introduction of *Window* in July 1943, the *Nachtjagd* was forced to adopt new, more flexible interception tactics dubbed *Zahme Sau* (Tame Boar). In order for the tactics to succeed, it was critical that the *Jäger*-Division staff in each sector quickly developed an accurate *Luftlage* (air picture). The German *Jägerleitoffizier* (fighter control officer [JLO]) used this information to determine when to order a scramble. Once in the air, the Bf 110s orbited a radio beacon in their sector, awaiting vectoring from the JLO. However, RAF jamming made it difficult for the JLO to determine the exact location of the bomber stream. If he JLO did locate the bomber stream, he could vector up to three Bf 110s toward it using *Y-Verfahren* VHF radio navigation. In turn, RAF Lancaster ABCs jammed communications between the Y-Stations, the JLO and the Bf 110s. A British VHF-jamming operation known as *Corona* also disrupted Luftwaffe nightfighter communications. The Bf 110G-4 also had the capability to hunt independently using its *Naxos* radar detector to home in on the Lancaster's H2S ground-mapping radar.

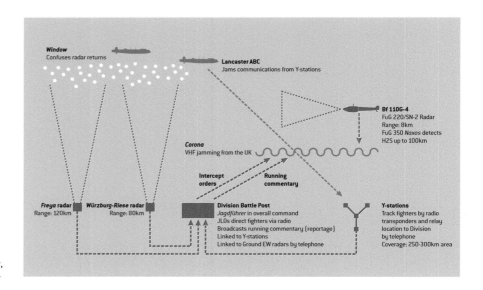

night navigation, was an essential prerequisite for the bomber stream. *Himmelbett* lacked the flexibility to re-deploy fighters from inactive sectors, so much of the *Nachtjagd* was left on the sidelines.

In response to the British overwhelming of the *Himmelbett* system, the subsequent introduction of *Window* and improved jamming of Luftwaffe C2, the *Nachtjagd* shifted to more de-centralised operational methods, dubbed *Zahme Sau* (Tame Boar), which enabled the Bf 110 *gruppen* to participate in a more free-play style than heretofore, while day fighters were also worked into the mix as *Wilde Sau* (Wild Boar).

Even though *Window* could make it difficult for the Germans to target individual Lancasters, the RAF could not hide the bomber stream itself. The Luftwaffe JLOs simply vectored their Bf 110s towards the largest radar returns, which they reasoned must be concealing bombers. Eventually, Bomber Command began using small diversionary raids to confuse the Germans, and after July 1943 the Lancaster versus Bf 110 duel was determined by the JLOs attempting to deduce the real target and vectoring their Bf 110s against the Main Force. Both sides upped the ante in August 1943, with the Luftwaffe introducing *Schräge Musik* upward-firing cannon, while Harris began to employ RAF 'intruder' units in support of his raids.

By the end of 1942, Bomber Command had greatly increased its ability to conduct night bombing, and Harris felt that he had the measure of his opponent. He laid great plans for 1943-44, intending to use his heavy bombers to break the back of the Third Reich with sustained assaults on Hamburg, the Ruhr and Berlin. The Luftwaffe's leadership also felt that it had gained the measure of Bomber Command, and that the *Nachtjagd* were ready and able to inflict catastrophic losses upon the RAF. In truth, the British held the strategic initiative in this duel but the Germans had a significant tactical edge.

THE COMBATANTS

LANCASTER AIRCREW TRAINING

Between November 1941 and May 1945, a total of 43 RAF, 15 Canadian, three Australian and one New Zealand squadrons were equipped with the Lancaster bomber. Lancaster units were normally divided into A and B flights, each of eight aircraft, for a total of 16 bombers. Each squadron also had two reserve Lancasters, which was increased to four in January 1944. Most squadrons had roughly 1.3 crews available for each aircraft, allowing for some rotation and ready replacements. However after the early war daylight formation tactics were abandoned, Lancaster crews were trained to operate and fight alone in the dark over hostile territory.

Before the war, the British had relied upon small service schools such as the RAF College Cranwell to train pilots and aircrew, but this system was insufficient to support the vast expansion that Bomber Command intended. Consequently, in December 1939, the Empire Air Training Scheme (EATS) was activated – a massive programme intended to train 49,300 aircrew from Great Britain, Canada, Australia and New Zealand each year. By late 1944 the EATS had trained more than 167,000 personnel, providing Bomber Command with a surplus of aircrews, despite heavy losses in 1943-44. The normal path for aircrew was for young men to volunteer for the RAF Volunteer Reserve (RAFVR), after which they would undergo four weeks of initial training. They would then be assigned a specific trade and proceed to other stations for specialised training. By 1943, the vast majority of Bomber Command aircrew were from the RAFVR.

Many Lancaster rear gunners removed the centre panels, but the freezing temperatures at high altitudes over Germany could make the occupant of the rear turret both lethargic and inattentive. Combat experience indicated that the rear gunner actually contributed little to the defence of the Lancaster, and that the best forms of protection for the bomber were speed and evasive tactics. (Imperial War Museum, CH 12776)

The Lancaster had a seven-man crew – pilot, flight engineer, navigator, bomb aimer, wireless operator, mid-upper gunner and rear gunner. Pilots began with ten months of basic flight training, moving from single-engined Tiger Moths to twin-engined Avro Ansons and, if successful, earning their wings. A critical aspect of their training was Beam Approach Training (BAT), which taught them the essential skill of how to land an aircraft at night using a radio-based blind-landing system. Navigators received 58 weeks of technical training, wireless operators 22 weeks and air gunners anywhere between seven and 18 weeks.

Having passed their basic courses, prospective aircrew would usually end up at a transit station such as Heaton Park near Manchester, before proceeding to an Operational Training Unit (OTU). The formation of a Lancaster crew began in the OTU, where the aircrew would informally begin aligning themselves into a team they could trust. After three weeks of ground classes, learning everything about their bomber's flight systems, weapons and controls, the newly-formed crew would begin an intensive ten-week flight training course on Wellington bombers, involving long-range navigation, high-level bombing and a limited amount of aerial gunnery. Only one-third of the flying during OTU courses was conducted at night. The crew would also undergo both day and night mock 'fighter attacks' from nearby RAF fighter units, to expose them to the suddenness of aerial combat. The OTU training culminated with a night bombing run on a simulated enemy city, complete with searchlights.

After the OTU, the crew would head to one of 14 Lancaster Heavy Conversion Units (HCUs), where they would fly the Avro bomber for six weeks. On some occasions, HCU units were committed to operational sorties over France in order to give new Lancaster crews a taste of actual combat conditions. Flying four-engined bombers at night proved difficult for many crews, and fatalities due to accidents and bad weather were quite heavy. Indeed the rate of attrition in training got so high that in late 1943 Bomber Command created four Lancaster Finishing Schools (LFSs) to add additional flight experience for new crews prior to them heading to an operational squadron.

In terms of preparing aircrew to fly long-range night sorties, the RAF training was quite good – it produced excellent crews, and in quantity, throughout the war. After spending a year or more in training, the Lancaster crews were comfortable with their aircraft, and its capabilities. However, the content of tactical training was often unrealistic compared to actual nightfighter threats. Gunnery training usually consisted of daylight firing of about 600 rounds (a two second-burst) at a target drogue towed directly behind the bomber, which had little in common with an attacking Bf 110 at night. Even worse, gunners were often warned not to fire their machine guns unless they were fired upon, since the muzzle flashes would give away the position of their aircraft – this discouraged them from firing at Bf 110s they had sighted first. Lancaster pilots were trained to use the corkscrew evasive tactic to counter nightfighter attacks from astern, and this manoeuvre was effective, but *Nachtjagd* pilots were familiar with this tactic and could anticipate it. Although Bomber Command became aware of the *Schräge Musik* tactic in March 1944, this information was withheld from Lancaster crews since there was no real counter to it.

Lancaster aircrew were very young, typically 18-22, and with only a year or two of military service under their belts. They knew that there was high risk attached to their profession, but many displayed the nonchalant attitude of one doomed aircrew member, who said, 'It's a sheer gamble in the game, but damn good fun while it lasts'. Initially, morale was very high in the newly converted Lancaster squadrons, since the aircraft was widely regarded as superior to all other RAF bombers. However, as losses began to mount in 1942-43, the morale across Bomber Command began to suffer and Lancaster crews were discouraged from trying to assess their personal odds for survival of a 25-sortie tour. Statistically, a sustained loss rate of just 3.3 per cent meant that no Lancaster aircrews would survive a standard 25-mission tour – Lancaster loss rates exceeded 3.3 per cent in six of twelve months both in 1942 and 1943. This of course assumed that Lancaster crews stuck it out, but during the costly Battle of Berlin a growing number of aircrew simply 'opted out' by refusing to fly, and accepting disciplinary measures.

Freeman Dyson, a civilian scientist working in Bomber Command's Operational Research Section, determined that experienced crews were just as likely to be shot down as inexperienced ones, which meant that survival usually came down to luck rather than skill. Over the course of the war, Bomber Command suffered a casualty rate of more than 61 per cent amongst its aircrew, with 44 per cent being killed – an extremely high rate of loss.

Bomber Command did receive the cream of Commonwealth manpower, and the Lancaster force was led by a number of very competent bomber pilots, such as Guy Gibson, Harold Martin, Willie Tait and Leonard Cheshire. However, the competence of individual Lancaster pilots generally had little impact on the Lancaster versus Bf 110 duel. One exception was Leonard Cheshire, who introduced a series of innovative tactics in No. 76 Sqn. He ordered the removal of the useless FN 5A nose and FN 50 mid-upper gun turrets, which increased the speed of the Lancaster and made it harder to intercept. Cheshire and a few other squadron commanders also experimented with low-level approaches, hiding their bombers from German radar in ground clutter, which often reduced losses. However, the majority of Bomber Command's aircrew employed the conventional tactics they had been taught, and suffered accordingly at the hands of German nightfighters.

Bf 110 AIRCREW TRAINING

While the majority of the German *Nachtjagd* aircrew in 1942-43 were also quite young, they had considerably more military experience than their RAF opponents flying Lancasters. Most Bf 110 pilots were 22-26 years old, although some of the more

successful *Nachtjäger* were in their early thirties. A large proportion of Bf 110 pilots had entered the Luftwaffe in 1937-39, and they represented a more pre-war professional cadre than the bulk of Bomber Command crews in 1942-45. A good number of *Nachtjäger* had previous daylight combat experience serving with *Zerstörer* units over Poland, Norway, France and Britain, while Major Günther Radusch was a *Legion Condor* veteran. Many Bf 110 crewmen came from diverse backgrounds prior to entering the Luftwaffe, including other parts of the Wehrmacht (infantry, panzers and flak crewmen), the Merchant Marine and Lufthansa commercial service. Initially, many pilots and aircrew from the *Zerstörergruppen* had been reluctant converts to the *Nachtjagd* role in 1940-41, since night flying was regarded as inherently more dangerous and less likely to produce a high-scoring career than day fighters. However, this attitude changed as Bf 110 crews saw the destruction Bomber Command inflicted on German cities. From 1942 many more volunteers came forward to defend the homeland.

Luftwaffe recruits spent six months in basic training at a *Fliegerersatzabteilung*, the best students being screened for pilot (*flugzeugführer*) training, while others were designated as radio operators (*bordfunker*) or flight mechanics (*bordmechaniker*). Up until 1943, the Luftwaffe invested an enormous effort in training its pilots, but it was only producing one-third as many as the RAF. Pilot training began at one of about 50 *Flugzeugführerschulen A/B*, such as Pilot School A/B 7 in Chemnitz. Candidates spent 11-12 months learning basic flight on single-engined biplanes such as the Focke-Wulf Fw 44 Stieglitz before eventually moving on to more demanding types such as the Arado Ar 96. Although all flight training at the A/B schools was conducted in daylight and during fair weather, there were still a significant number of accidents and casualties. At the conclusion of this period the successful candidate was awarded his A- and B-licenses, after which he was sent to one of 19 *Luftkriegschulen*, such as Air War School 1 in Dresden.

The purpose of the *Luftkriegschulen* was to begin transforming the fledgling pilot into a Luftwaffe officer, with classes on tactics, military law and other relevant subjects. During this period, if not before, instructors would determine if the pilot was best suited for single or multi-engined aircraft, and if selected for service with a Bf 110 unit, the pilot would continue on to a *Flugzeugführerschule* C after a few months of classroom

1. Direction finder
2. Dead reckoning compass repeater
3. Clock
4. Light switches
5. Compass deviation card
6. Engine ignition switches (x4)
7. Engine starter switches (x4)
8. Stopwatch
9. Airspeed indicator
10. Artificial horizon
11. Rate-of-climb indicator
12. Boost gauges (x4)
13. IFF
14. IFF switch
15. Bomb containers jettison button
16. Bomb jettison button
17. Beam approach indicator
18. Brake lever
19. Steering yoke
20. Turn-and-bank indicator
21. Engine tachometers (x4)
22. Vacuum pump suction gauge
23. Vacuum pump changeover cock
24. Oxygen regulator control
25. Oxygen regulator gauge
26. Undercarriage position indicator
27. Control column
28. Throttle control levers (x4)
29. Flap position indicator
30. Supercharger gear-change control panel
31. Propeller feathering buttons (x4)
32. Triple brake pressure gauge
33. Magnetic compass
34. Auto controls pressure gauge
35. Signalling key for formation keeping
36. Master engine cocks (x4)
37. Engine fire extinguisher buttons (x4)
38. Signalling switches
39. Rudder pedals (x2)
40. Propeller control speed levers (x4)
41. Control levers friction adjusters (x2)
42. Radiator shutter controls
43. Pilot's intercom box
44. Jump seat
45. Auto controls cock
46. Auto controls clutch
47. Cockpit lights (x2)
48. Rudder/elevator trim controls
49. Pilot's seat
50. Seat adjustment lever
51. Mixer box
52. Beam approach control unit
53. Autopilot master lever
54. Pilot's call light
55. Auto controls altitude control unit

Early-build Lancaster B Is of No. 49 Sqn await sunset on the dispersal strip at Scampton, in Lincolnshire, in late 1942. Prior to a raid, Lancaster crews would test their radios on the ground, which often alerted Luftwaffe signal intercept personnel that a raid was scheduled for that night. This operational-level early warning gave the Luftwaffe the time it needed to deploy Bf 110s in likely air approach corridors. (Imperial War Museum, CH 9134)

instruction at the *Luftkriegschulen*. The C-school was designed to strengthen navigational skills and introduce the pilot to flying a twin-engined aircraft at night and in all weather conditions. The heart of the curricula of the C-school was getting the pilot comfortable with instrument flying, which was an essential prerequisite for service in the *Nachtjagd staffel*. If successful, after several months of flying the pilot would receive his C-licence for multi-engined aircraft. If selected for the *Nachtjagd*, the pilot would then proceed to *Nachtjagdschule* 1 (Nightfighter School) at Schleissheim, near Munich. Here, the pilot teamed up with a *bordfunker* and began converting either to the Bf 110, Ju 88G or Do 217. Night combat training was highly realistic, and in addition to more complicated night navigation and instrument flying, the pilot learned how to execute GCI missions guided by a Luftwaffe controller. However, the shortage of fuel was already affecting flight training in early 1942, and future 59-victory ace Paul Zorner noted that he logged only 16.5 hours at night out of 72 hours total while at *Nachtjagdschule* 1.

After *Nachtjagdschule* 1, the pilot would be assigned to a specific *Nachtjagdgeschwader*, and he would proceed to its *Ergänzungsgruppe* (replacement) unit. For example, NJG 1's *Ergänzungsgruppe* was located in Stuttgart in 1942. Typically, in 1941-43 Bf 110 nightfighter pilots received about 160-200 hours of flight experience before reaching their operational *staffel*. However, by 1943 fuel shortages began biting into the Luftwaffe's training programme, causing a reduction in flight hours. The Demyansk and Stalingrad airlifts also severely disrupted the Luftwaffe's training programme by siphoning off pilots and aircraft for logistical support in the USSR. Finally, Allied bomber raids over Germany forced Göring to commit training units directly into defensive combat in 1944, which effectively de-railed the training programme.

Most of the *Flugzeugführerschulen* C were disbanded after D-Day and new pilots simply went from an abbreviated A/B training school directly to a replacement unit, where they would receive a hasty course in flying a Bf 110 at night on instruments. Training accidents rose sharply in 1944, while pilot quality fell to unacceptable levels. The only thing that saved the *Nachtjagd* from complete dissolution after mid-1944 was the fact that night combat losses remained fairly low (much lower than for Luftwaffe daylight fighter pilots), allowing a hardened core of skilled pilots to fight on to the end.

Yet no matter how skilled a Bf 110 pilot became, he ultimately depended upon his *bordfunker* to find their target and direct him towards it. Unlike day combat,

Bf 110G-4 COCKPIT

1. Fuel cock levers (x2)
2. Seat adjustment handle
3. Throttle levers (x2)
4. Electrical system cutout switch
5. Fuel system priming pump levers (x2)
6. Magneto switches (x2)
7. Undercarriage and flap emergency operation switches (x2)
8. Flap control switches
9. Air pressure gauge
10. Propeller pitch control levers
11. Undercarriage controls
12. Undercarriage position indicator
13. Cockpit illumination (x6)

14. Repeater compass
15. Autopilot
16. Control column and gun-firing button
17. Altimeter
18. Cannon rounds indicator
19. Machine gun rounds indicator
20. Front cockpit locking levers (x3)
21. Turn and bank indicator
22. Revi gunsight
23. Artificial horizon
24. Port coolant temperature indicator
25. Fuel contents gauge
26. Starboard coolant temperature indicator

27. Coolant radiator flap position selector (port)
28. Fuel tank selector switch
29. Coolant radiator flap position selector (starboard)
30. Airspeed indicator
31. Rate-of-climb indicator
32. Main switch for autopilot
33. Exterior temperature gauge
34. Port RPM indicator
35. Starboard RPM indicator
36. Port boost gauge
37. Starboard boost gauge
38. Rudder pedals (x2)
39. Compass
40. Oxygen pressure gauge
41. Dimmer switch
42. Rudder trim control lever

43. Starter handles (x2)
44. Oxygen control
45. Spark plug cleaning handles
46. Selector lever for tank replenishing pump
47. Pilot's seat
48. Elevator trim control
49. Clock
50. FuG 10 radio altimeter
51. AFN 2 homing indicator
52. Mechanical or auto propeller pitch controls
53. Cockpit heat control
54. Emergency autopilot switch
55. Ammunition rounds indicators (x2)

JOHN DERING NETTLETON

John Dering Nettleton was born in Nongoma, Natal, South Africa, on 28 June 1917. Nettleton's family had a strong Royal Navy heritage, with his father being a captain and his grandfather an admiral. John was educated at a preparatory school in Cape Town in anticipation of him following his father's path into the Royal Navy. However, John proved to be an indifferent student, and when he applied to the Royal Naval College at Dartmouth in 1930 he failed the entrance exam. John returned to South Africa and spent nearly three years training as a naval cadet in Cape Town. However, after completing his training, he spent two years in the merchant marine, and later worked ashore as a civil engineer.

Bored with mundane tasks in Cape Town, the 21-year-old John Nettleton decided to return to England in late 1938 to make another attempt at starting a military career. He decided to try the RAF, which was less interested in academic qualifications, and he was accepted into the RAFVR for pilot training in December 1938. When World War II commenced, Nettleton had not yet completed his flight training. Upon receiving his wings he was assigned to No. 207 Sqn (a training unit equipped with Fairey Battle light bombers). In 1940, Nettleton was briefly assigned to two more training squadrons, but he did not see any active service with Bomber Command until he was transferred to No. 44 Sqn in June 1941. Roughly a quarter of the aircrew in this squadron were of Rhodesian origin, and Nettleton fitted in well. Like other later Lancaster pilots such as Guy Gibson, Nettleton gained his first combat experience flying the twin-engined Handley Page Hampden. In late 1941, No. 44 Sqn was designated to become the first Bomber Command unit to receive the new Lancaster bomber, and Nettleton was one of the first to train on it.

When Harris decided to mount the low-level daylight raid against the M.A.N. diesel engine plant in Augsburg, Bavaria, Nettleton was made an acting squadron leader and put in command of the six Lancasters from his squadron. Taking off at 1500 hrs on 17 April 1942, Nettleton led his six Lancasters at extremely low-level across France, but four bombers were quickly shot down by Fw 190As and Bf 109Fs from II./JG 2. Pressing on across more than 500 miles of enemy territory, Nettleton reached Augsburg with the other surviving bomber and they dropped their bombs on the target. The other Lancaster was shot down by flak and Nettleton's aircraft

was riddled with shrapnel, but he managed to nurse it back home in the dark, the sole surviving Lancaster from his squadron. Bomber Command was impressed with Nettleton's bravery and 'press-on' leadership, and awarded him the Victoria Cross. After the raid, Nettleton was interviewed by the BBC, and he said that, 'We Lancaster crews believe that in the Lancaster we have got the answer for heavy bombing'. Later, Nettleton took leave to marry and was then sent on a publicity tour to the United States.

Nettleton returned to No. 44 Sqn later in 1942, and continued as its leader for more than a year. On the night of 12/13 July 1943, Sqn Ldr Nettleton flew his Lancaster on a mission to Turin, in Italy, but on the return leg, he was apparently intercepted by a Bf 110 nightfighter and shot down over the Bay of Biscay. Nettleton and the Lancaster's remaining seven crew were all killed. Nettleton was typical of the aggressive Lancaster bomber pilots in 1942-43, impressed by the capabilities of their aircraft, and believing that 'the bomber would always get through'. (Photo of Sqn Ldr John D Nettleton courtesy of the author.)

MARTIN DREWES

Martin Drewes was born in October 1918 in a small village in Hanover, three weeks before the Armistice that ended World War I. When he reached 19, Drewes began his military service with the army by enrolling as an officer cadet with *Panzer-Regiment* 6 in November 1937. He spent nearly two years in the army, commanding a PzKw I tank and receiving his commission just before the start of the war. In September 1939, Drewes transferred to the Luftwaffe and received his A/B licences in April 1940, followed by *Zerstörer* training at Schleissheim. In February 1941, Drewes was assigned to 4./ZG 76 near Wilhelmshaven as a *Zerstörer* pilot. After three uneventful months flying defensive patrols over the North Sea, Drewes' unit was briefly transferred to Greece and then his *staffel* was assigned to *Fliegerführer Irak* in May 1941. Drewes flew his Bf 110 to Vichy-held Syria and then to Iraq, where the Axis-supported uprising fell apart very quickly. However, Drewes did score his first victory over Iraq – an RAF Gloster Gladiator biplane fighter – before returning with ZG 76 to Holland.

After many tiresome patrols over the North Sea, Drewes shot down a Spitfire in August 1941, which demonstrated his exceptional skill as a Bf 110 pilot. In November his squadron was re-designated as 7./NJG 3, and Drewes found himself in the *Nachtjagd*. After a brief transition to nightfighters, he was involved in providing air cover over the Channel Dash in February 1942, and was then briefly stationed in Norway to protect the battleship *Tirpitz*. Drewes' career as a Bf 110 nightfighter pilot began in earnest during the Battle of Berlin, when he shot down a Stirling in January 1943. Initially, Drewes scored slowly, getting only two more kills over the next seven months, including a Lancaster in June 1943. He achieved four more kills in August-September 1943 and shot down three American bombers in January 1944, but the war was approaching its final year and he still had achieved only modest success.

In March 1944 Hauptmann Drewes was appointed commander of III./NJG 1, and he would remain in control of this unit until May 1945. Opportunities to score victories in the *Nachtjagd* were often dependent upon location, and as *Gruppenkommandeur*, Drewes could ensure that he would be in the thick of the action. He was involved in intercepting the bomber stream during the Nurnberg raid in March 1944, and shot down three Lancasters that night. Drewes downed a total of five Lancasters in March, six in April and 14 in May.

His best night came on 4 May 1944, when he shot down five Lancasters with his *Schräge Musik* during the raid on Mailly-le-Camp. During one attack using *Schräge Musik*, Drewes' Bf 110G-4 was damaged by debris from an exploding Lancaster, forcing him and his *bordfunker* to bail out. He shot down another five Lancasters in June-July and was awarded the *Ritterkreuz* (Knight's Cross) on 27 July.

Drewes was promoted to major in December 1944, but his active career was winding down and he scored only a single victory in the last six months of the war – a Lancaster on 3 March 1945. He was awarded the *Eichenlaub* (Oak Leaves) just before the end of the war. Major Drewes managed to survive 235 missions in the *Nachtjagd*, and surrendered to the British. He had scored a total of 52 victories, including at least 33 Lancasters. After a brief stint in captivity, Drewes was released and moved to Brazil in 1947. Here, he worked as a pilot and later as a businessman. Now aged 94, Martin Drewes lives in retirement in Brazil. (Photo of Major Martin Drewes courtesy of the author.)

A *bordfunker* exiting the rear cockpit of a Bf 110. As more and more electronic equipment was added into Bf 110 nightfighters, the *bordfunker* evolved from being the simple radio operator of 1940-41 into a highly technical electronic warfare specialist of 1943-45. The success of individual Bf 110 crews was increasingly dependent upon the skill of the *bordfunker* to find Lancasters amid an intense jamming environment. (Bundesarchiv, Bild 101I-658-6395-005, Foto: Hebenstreit)

intercepting and shooting down Lancaster bombers at night was a two-man operation. Enlisted personnel with technical skills or those recruits who failed at some level of pilot training were given the option to became radio/radar operators on Bf 110s. After receiving both gunnery and signals training in various Luftwaffe schools, a *bordfunker* would receive specialised training on the FuG 202 or later model radars at a facility run by Telefunken. Since electronic equipment aboard the Bf 110G-4 evolved so rapidly between 1942 and 1944, even skilled *bordfunker* had to continually receive updated training to stay abreast of new technology. In active squadrons, pilots used rank and status to get paired with the most skilled *bordfunker*, since they knew that this would determine their success against RAF bombers. Some Bf 110 nightfighters also carried a *bordmechaniker*, but this became increasingly difficult as more equipment such as *Schräge Musik* was added in the cockpit.

Luftwaffe *Nachtjäger* were essentially divided into three groups. The first group consisted of the best and most aggressive pilots, combined with a competent *bordfunker*, who regularly scored kills. The second group consisted of above average aircrew who scored occasionally, but only under optimal conditions. The third, and largest, group by far consisted of average or mediocre aircrew, who never scored a single victory. Younger pilots complained that *Himmelbett* favoured a handful of senior pilots getting the best sectors to score, while junior pilots were often held in reserve. The introduction of *Zahme Sau* opened up the playing field to everyone, which created a whole new crop of Bf 110 aces. However, the key difference between Bf 110 aircrew and their Lancaster opponents was that the *Nachtjäger* were serving for the duration, not limited to a 25-mission tour.

COMBAT

Unlike the USAAF's daylight bombing campaign of Germany, which pitted large formations of American heavy bombers against large groups of Luftwaffe day fighters, most of Bomber Command's night combat actions throughout 1941-44 saw a single bomber targeted by a solitary nightfighter. Although hundreds of aircraft were involved in the larger aerial battles, like those fought around Nurnberg in March 1944, the tactical dynamic of Lancaster versus Bf 110 aerial combat was usually limited to one-on-one actions.

INITIAL SKIRMISHES, 1942

Although a handful of Lancasters participated in RAF night raids on Essen and Lübeck in March 1942, it was not until Operation *Millennium* – the '1,000-bomber' Cologne Raid on 30/31 May 1942 – that a sizeable number of Lancasters attacked targets in Germany. During the operation No. 5 Group despatched 73 Lancasters, of which one was lost to flak. Harris introduced the bomber stream for the first time during Operation *Millennium*, which caught NJG 1 by surprise with too few aeroplanes in the air at the outset of the raid. Normally, a *Nachtjagd staffel* would launch fighters progressively during the night, since the previous British de-centralised tactics had seen Bomber Command take up to four hours to move 80-150 bombers through a *Himmelbett* zone, but now more than 1,000 bombers passed through in just 90 minutes. Most of the Bf 110s did not get into the fight until after bombs had already begun falling on Cologne, even though they did manage to shoot down about 20 RAF bombers on their return run – the best night yet in the air war for the *Nachtjagd*.

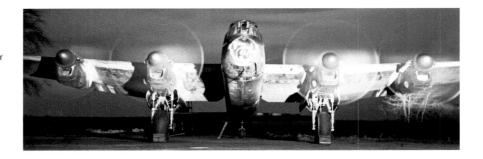

In addition to the Augsburg raid, Harris tried three other daylight, low-level missions with all-Lancaster forces against Danzig, Milan and the Le Creusot factory in France. Except for the Augsburg raid, the Luftwaffe was caught by surprise by these daring low-level operations and failed to intercept the attacking force. Despite the Lancaster's demonstrated ability to conduct successful penetration missions at low-level in daylight – indicating the limitations of German radar coverage – Harris decided that his Lancasters should revert to the night bombing role at medium-high altitudes. However, some Lancaster squadrons continued to experiment with low-level tactics, particularly when returning from targets at night.

The first proper encounter between the Lancaster and the Bf 110 at night occurred over Waterloo, in Belgium, on the night of 2/3 June 1942, when Oberfeldwebel Fritz Schellwat of 5./NJG 1 managed to find a Lancaster bomber and shoot it down. A few more Bf 110 interceptions of Lancasters occurred during the rest of the summer, but the most significant action took place on the night of 29/30 July when Bomber Command attacked Saarbrücken. When German ground-based radars spotted the British bomber stream, Oberleutnant Reinhold Eckardt, a veteran pilot and *staffel* leader of 7./NJG 3, took off in his Bf 110E-2 and managed to shoot down a Stirling and Halifax. Directed southwest of Brussels by his JLO, Eckardt spotted a Lancaster from No. 50 Sqn and conducted a successful rear attack that shot it down. Elated by three kills in one night, Eckardt closed in on another Lancaster, but in this case an alert rear gunner spotted him first and sprayed his Bf 110E-2 with machine gun fire, damaging an engine. Eckardt and his *bordfunker* were forced to bail out, but his parachute caught on the Bf 110's tail and he went down with his aeroplane. Not only was this the first occasion of a Lancaster shooting down a Bf 110, but the Lancaster gunner had ended the career of a 19-victory Luftwaffe ace.

By late July No. 5 Group had sufficient operational Lancasters to send 113 against Dusseldorf on the night of 31 July/1 August 1942, and lost only two. This lucky streak continued for three weeks until 24/25 August, when No. 5 Group sent 61 Lancasters to participate in a raid on Frankfurt, but lost six aircraft (nearly ten per cent of those involved), including three shot down by Bf 110s from NJG 1. Over the next several nights the *Nachtjagd* inflicted serious losses on raids on Kassel and Nurnberg, including seven Lancasters (two by Bf 110s from NJG 1). While these overall losses were still fairly light, they represented a cumulative nine per cent loss rate over three medium-sized raids. Although Kammhuber stuck with the static *Himmelbett* system, he also began to send Bf 110s aloft to orbit near Y-station radio beacons until the *Nachtjäger* division staffs could determine what route the bomber stream was using that night. Once the location of the bomber stream was determined, JLOs would vector in waiting fighters to attack. These more decentralised tactics, known as *Dunkel Nachtjagd* (Dark Night Hunting), threatened the bombers over a longer part of their mission, and enabled Kammhuber to mass more fighters than the previous *Himmelbett* system had allowed. Consequently, bomber losses began to increase late in 1942 as the *Nachtjagd* adopted new tactics. Lancaster operations also began to ramp up in November-December 1942, with raids against Hamburg, Stuttgart, the Ruhr and Munich, but losses were noticeably heavier than in the spring and summer months. Using *Dunkel Nachtjagd*, the Bf 110s were able to shoot down ten Lancasters in December, although the number of fighters engaging bombers was still relatively small.

Alerted that the British are on the way, a radarless Bf 110 is prepared for take-off. Without onboard radar, aircraft such as this one were forced to operate near searchlight zones, hoping to spot a passing Lancaster. (Bundesarchiv, Bild 101I-658-6360-07, Foto: Helmut Grosse)

In one bizarre incident over the Ruhr, a Lancaster rear gunner who came under attack from a Bf 110F-4 bailed out and fell right into one of the nightfighter's propellers. The gunner's body bent the propeller and forced the pilot to shut down an engine. After making an emergency landing, the crew discovered fragments of the Lancaster gunner on the FuG 202 radar antennae. This unfortunate crewman came closer to eliminating a Bf 110 than most Lancaster gunners.

During 1942, Bomber Command conducted about 4,900 Lancaster sorties, which represented 14 per cent of its total effort for that year. No fewer than 167 Lancasters were lost, including at least 26 shot down by Bf 110s and seven by other nightfighters. More Lancasters had been destroyed by flak and crash-landings then *Nachtjagd* action, so Bomber Command still had little reason to regard nightfighters as the primary threat. Overall, the Lancasters suffered a 3.4 per cent attrition rate in 1942. The other two British heavy bombers, the Stirling and Halifax, suffered heavier losses and proved less capable than the Lancaster, so Harris was eager to make the latter type the key weapon system in Bomber Command. While the twin-engined Wellington was still predominant in numbers, the older Whitley and Hampden bombers had been retired from Bomber Command by mid-1942, and Harris intended that four-engined bombers would comprise the bulk of his forces by mid-1943. On the German side, the *Nachtjagd* had lost about 50 Bf 110s in combat in 1942, but far more to collisions and friendly flak, with only a handful downed by Lancaster gunners.

BLOODBATH, 1943-44

Bomber Command's No. 8 Group began experimenting with early Pathfinder operations over the Ruhr in January 1943, supporting raids by 50-60 Lancasters from No. 5 Group. The *Nachtjagd* were easily able to mass against these small formations, and Bf 110s shot down 11 Lancasters in ten days. The pilots from both NJGs 1 and 3 became increasingly skilled at picking off Lancasters, but the growing lethality of *Nachtjagd* defences was not apparent until Bomber Command launched two major raids against Berlin on 16-17 January 1943.

The first raid caught the Luftwaffe by surprise, and Bomber Command lost only a single Lancaster out of the 190 despatched. However, Harris inexplicably sent the bomber stream along the same route the next night, and this time the *Nachtjagd* were waiting. At least 14 Bf 110s from NJGs 1 and 3 got in amongst the bombers and shot 11 Lancasters down out of 170 on the raid. Eight more Avro bombers were lost to other causes, including flak, resulting in the raiders suffering a loss rate of more than 11 per cent. This Berlin raid was the first major success for the Bf 110s against the Lancasters.

In February 1943 the Germans acquired an intact H2S radar from a downed bomber, and it was quickly handed over to Telefunken for technical analysis. Once its engineers had learned the characteristics of the H2S, Telefunken was able to advise the *Funkhorchdienst* on how to detect its emissions. The RAF remained unaware of this German intelligence coup (although it should have been assumed), and Bomber Command continued to allow its bombers to test H2S on the ground prior to a raid. The *Funkhorchdienst* monitored H2S transmissions, using them to provide early warning of impending raids to the Bf 110 units. Yet the RAF was not completely asleep, as its own electronic specialists learned the frequency of the FuG 202 radar in December 1942.

In March 1943 Harris decided to direct his steadily increasing force of four-engined heavy bombers against targets in the Ruhr. No. 8 Group Pathfinders were now equipped with H2S mapping radar, which Harris believed would improve bombing accuracy over the notoriously overcast Ruhr industrial area. However, Kammhuber also had a greater number of nightfighters available, including the improved Bf 110G-4. Crews flying this aircraft with NJG 1, NJG 3 and the new NJG 4 were able to shoot down 19 Lancasters in March, 34 in April and 36 in May. During any given raid, the trend was still for one Bf 110 pilot to score one victory against a Lancaster, not multiple kills by a single pilot. In addition, another 113 Lancasters were lost in the same period to flak and other causes.

With most of the Ju 88 nightfighters of NJG 2 having been transferred to the Mediterranean theatre, the Bf 110s were carrying virtually the entire fight against Bomber Command at this point. A total of 60 Bf 110 nightfighters were lost during March-May 1943, of which 21 were as a result of combat – possibly as many as four of these were lost attacking Lancasters. Based upon these actions, Bf 110 crews were achieving a victory-to-loss rate of more than 20-to-1 over the Lancaster. Yet despite this optimistic picture for the *Nachtjagd*, the relative combat advantage could change suddenly. On 9 May 1943, a traitorous German crew from 10./NJG 3 handed Bomber Command a plum when they flew

A Bf 110 attacked this Lancaster from No. 57 Sqn over Germany on the night of 14/15 June 1943, killing the rear gunner with 20mm cannon fire. Next, the German pilot sprayed the bomber's fuselage with machine gun fire, knocking out the radio and navigational equipment. However, the fighter was unable to finish off the damaged bomber, which made it home to Scampton. (Imperial War Museum, CE 76)

their Ju 88R-1 nightfighter to Scotland, providing British scientists at the TRE with an intact FuG 202 *Lichtenstein* radar to study. This defection greatly assisted the British in developing *Window* to defeat the FuG 202. The scientists at TRE also developed the *Serrate* passive receiving device, which could detect FuG 202 emissions at distances of up to 80km away. Fighter Command began installing *Serrate* on its Beaufighter nightfighters to hunt down Bf 110s equipped with the FuG 202.

In June 1943, Bomber Command conducted nine major raids against the Ruhr, culminating in the massive attack on Cologne. NJG 1's Bf 110s bore the brunt of the defensive battle, shooting down 207 RAF bombers, including 89 Lancasters. Now that NJG 1 had a stable of veteran nightfighter pilots, the lethality of *Nachtjagd* attacks increased dramatically, and multiple kills became more frequent. Eight different Bf 110 pilots from NJG 1 were able to shoot down two or more Lancasters in a single night during June 1943, with Hauptmann Manfred Meuer setting the new standard by destroying three Lancasters on 15 June and going one better two nights later. All told, the *Nachtjagd* destroyed nearly one-third of Bomber Command's frontline strength in just a month, and took 1,600 RAF aircrew out of the war. In return, NJG 1 lost just eight Bf 110s in combat and ten to other causes, or 16 per cent of its available Bf 110s. Furthermore, most of the German aircrew that were shot down would survive to fight again. Oberfeldwebel Fritz Schellwat of 5./NJG 1 – the Bf 110 pilot who downed the first Lancaster bomber – was himself shot down by return fire from a Lancaster over the Ruhr in June 1943, but he survived the war. Altogether, at least three Bf 110s were lost in combat with Lancasters, meaning that the exchange ratio had risen to about 30-to-1 in the Germans' favour.

Although Harris was satisfied with the bombing damage inflicted on the Ruhr in June 1943, which included the death of 4,377 Germans on the ground, the statistics indicate that the *Nachtjagd* was gaining a decisive edge in the air battle over Germany. At this rate it was clear to almost everyone but Harris that morale in Bomber Command would break long before German home front morale.

While unwilling to admit failure in the Battle of the Ruhr – German morale was still intact and armament production steadily increasing – Harris could see that it was time to revise his tactics. He finally gained permission from the Air Ministry to use *Window* operationally, and he intended to employ it on a massive scale on his next campaign – a series of major attacks against Hamburg. On the night of 24/25 July 1943, 791 RAF bombers were sent to attack Hamburg. As they approached the target they began dropping bundles of 27cm-long *Window* throughout the bomber stream – the length of the aluminium strips was specifically designed to provide false returns for the *Freya* and *Würzburg* ground-based radars. *Himmelbett* was effectively blinded and the FuG 202 *Lichtenstein* radar aboard Bf 110s in the air was also impaired. At one stroke, Bomber Command ruined the Luftwaffe's *Luftlage* (air situation) reporting over Germany, which deprived the Bf 110 crews of their ability to find and attack the bombers. *Window* caught the *Nachtjagd* totally by surprise, and it caused so much confusion that the bombers were able to strike Hamburg and return with little interference from the Luftwaffe. Only 12 bombers, including four Lancasters, were lost – a loss rate of just 1.5 per cent. Harris followed up with three more raids on Hamburg between 27 July and 3 August, precipitating the infamous 'firestorm' that killed in excess of 40,000 German civilians.

A Luftwaffe fighter direction centre. The effectiveness of the *Nachtjagd* depended heavily upon centralised command and control, which was eventually disrupted by Allied jamming. (Author)

Although the introduction of *Window* temporarily swung the aerial duel in Bomber Command's favour, the *Nachtjagd* moved quickly to regain the initiative through tactical and technological approaches. German radar operators noted the differences between moving aircraft and clouds of *Window* on their screens, which enabled the more skilled JLOs to guess the approximate location of the bomber stream and direct their nightfighters towards it. British losses began to rise up to four per cent on the last two Hamburg raids. All told, the Battle of Hamburg cost Bomber Command 87 bombers, including 39 Lancasters. The Bf 110s were briefly reduced to near impotence, accounting for only about a dozen of the Lancasters. Even before the Battle of Hamburg had ended the Luftwaffe attempted to counter *Window* through the introduction of more fluid *Wilde Sau* tactics in place of *Himmelbett*. Henceforth, *Nachtjagd* pilots would take off when alerted and circle a radio beacon until vectored towards the estimated RAF target city by JLOs. A running commentary would be issued on multiple radio frequencies to keep airborne Bf 110s informed about enemy locations and their likely target. Unlike the previous *Himmelbett* system, where individual Bf 110 *staffel* only operated over a small area, *Wilde Sau* enabled the *Nachtjagd* to mass its forces, but it required much more navigational skill, and initiative, on the part of Bf 110 pilots to ensure success. And *Wilde Sau* was a very risky tactic as its exposed nightfighters to friendly flak, as well as possible collisions with other Luftwaffe aircraft.

Just as the *Nachtjagd* was attempting to adjust to a new tactical method to mitigate the RAF's use of *Window*, Bomber Command sortied almost 600 bombers, including 324 Lancasters, against the German rocket research facility at Peenemünde on the night of 17/18 August 1943. A large Intruder operation was mounted in support of the raid, with *Serrate*-equipped Beaufighters shooting down four Bf 110s from NJG 1, including aircraft flown by two aces. Meanwhile, the raiding force unexpectedly approached the target across Denmark – dropping *Window* along the way – and employed a Mosquito diversionary force against Berlin, which helped confuse the *Nachtjagd's Luftlage*. Most of the 158 nightfighters scrambled at around 2030 hrs were mistakenly sent towards Berlin, leaving Peenemünde virtually unprotected. A few Bf 110s from NJG 3 conducted four intercepts as the bombers crossed Denmark, but failed to shoot down any bombers. Consequently, Bomber Command was able to hit the target for 30 minutes without any interference from the Luftwaffe. Eventually, individual Bf 110 pilots circling Berlin realised that they had been deceived, and those who were not low on fuel headed north towards Peenemünde. Although the German nightfighters arrived piecemeal, they found ideal conditions due to a bright moon, cloudless sky and illumination from fires on the ground. Bf 110 pilots could easily spot the bomber stream at much greater range than normal and did not require their radar, so the use of *Window* had little or no effect on them.

At 0140 hrs on 18 August, the German nightfighters began slashing into the final wave of RAF bombers attacking Peenemünde – the Lancasters of No. 5 Group and Halifaxes of No. 6 Group. In an intense 50-minute-long aerial battle, 18 Lancasters were shot down. One of the first Bf 110 pilots to engage was a combat novice, Leutnant Dieter Musset of 5./NJG 1. His *bordfunker*, Obergefreiter Helmut Hafner, noted that, 'we picked up the first one by radar, but the rest were all spotted visually by Leutnant Musset. His method was to climb after each attack, because the Messerschmitt 110 was comparatively slow, and make the next attack in a shallow dive. He was able to see the bombers' exhausts from above'.

Despite lacking prior combat experience, Musset succeeded in shooting down a Lancaster and four Halifaxes, thus becoming an ace in just 14 minutes. However, his luck ran out when he attacked a Lancaster from No. 619 Sqn, flown by Sgt R. T. Hughes. Due to the bright moonlight, Musset could clearly see the bombers, but that worked both ways. The rear and mid-upper gunners spotted his Bf 110 and fired 1,000 rounds of 0.303in. ammunition at him.

A Luftwaffe mechanic points out a 0.303in. bullet hole in a Bf 110's DB 601 engine block. Although the *Zerstörer's* cockpit and windscreen had some armoured protection, its engines were vulnerable to machine gun fire. Yet it is interesting to note that this Bf 110 made it back to base despite engine damage, proving once again that 0.303in. rounds lacked the destructive power to consistently destroy enemy aircraft. (Author)

On the receiving end, Hafner stated that, 'it hit us and we were in too much trouble to watch it [the Lancaster]. We had been hit by a burst of machine gun fire, which started a fire in our port engine and I was hit by an incendiary bullet in my shoulder. We turned away from the bomber stream and tried to reach Güstrow airfield, but the fire spread, we lost control and both of us had to bail out.'[1]

Oberleutnant Paul Zorner from 7./NJG 3 shot down two Lancasters using the standard *unten den hinten* method. He stated that, 'I closed up on him carefully and recognised it as a Lancaster. At about 120m I opened fire – just one burst. I hit him in the right wing between the engines, as that was the most sensitive point. It started to burn'. Zorner noted that he received no return fire, and that the Lancaster failed to take evasive action. Ten minutes later Zorner polished off another Lancaster that failed to fire back or evade. Zorner concluded that, 'I don't think he ever saw me.'[2]

A watershed in the Bf 110 versus Lancaster duel occurred when two Bf 110G-4s from 5./NJG 5, equipped with experimental *Schräge Musik* upward-firing cannon, joined the battle around Peenemünde. Leutnant Peter Erhardt, another pilot with limited previous night combat experience, used *Schräge Musik* to destroy four Lancasters in 20 minutes. However, the other Bf 110 equipped with *Schräge Musik*, flown by Unteroffizier Walter Hölker, shot down a Lancaster but was then spotted by another Lancaster and the German pilot wounded as a result of return fire by the tail gunner. Since the 20mm cannon in *Schräge Musik* did not use tracers, surviving RAF bomber crews remained ignorant about the source of these attacks. Historian Martin Middlebrook calculated that 46 separate aerial engagements occurred during this 50-minute battle, resulting in the loss of 28 bombers and five nightfighters (four Bf 110s and one Do 217). Based upon the data from this action, a Lancaster only had a 40 per cent chance of surviving if engaged, while a Bf 110 had a 90 per cent chance of surviving. It is important to note

1   Martin Middlebrook, *The Peenemunde Raid* (London, Cassel & Co., 1982), pp. 161-162.
2   Middlebrook, pp. 163-164

however, that the visibility was unusually good during the aerial battle around Peenemünde, and that British gunners were on high alert over the target area.

Yet as the RAF bombers turned for home after targeting Peenemünde, most of the nightfighters had to break off due to low fuel. The Lancaster crews of No. 5 Group settled back for the long flight home across the North Sea and ceased dropping *Window*. From behind, a lone Bf 110, flown by Feldwebel Hans Meissner of 6./NJG 3 approached unseen. Meissner had taken off later than the rest of his *staffel* and had missed the battle over Peenemünde, but now he was the only German nightfighter still capable of action. His *bordfunker* noted:

Suddenly, I picked up a lot of contacts on my Lichtenstein radar. There were at least five contacts, all clear ones. I guided the pilot to the first and, at about 200m, he told me he'd got it. He'd seen it. It was a Lancaster. Meissner closed up to within about 50m of the bomber – below and behind – opened fire and hit the right inner engine. It exploded after just one burst of fire, and large chunks of that engine broke off. We banked and watched it falling down in flames, and saw it explode on the ground.

Meissner shot down three Lancasters in 15 minutes. None of the bombers returned fire or tried to evade. None of their 21 crewmen survived. Overall, No. 5 Group's Lancasters had suffered a crippling 14.5 per cent loss rate on the Peenemünde raid, but the German loss of eight Bf 110s was also quite heavy.

Less than a week later Harris began the Battle of Berlin with a raid by more than 700 bombers against the German capital on 23/24 August. Harris believed that his heavy bombers could bring the Third Reich to its knees by devastating its capital, and he measured success by dropping the 'magic' number of 40,000 tons of bombs on the capital. Harris was using the Lancasters to execute a counter-value strategy, with their target being German civilians. However, the Bf 110s were tasked to conduct a counter-force mission, with success measured by shooting down British bombers. Harris' mistake in the Battle of Berlin was in failing to recognise that the *Nachtjagd* was no longer tied to *Himmelbett* boxes, which meant that it could mass its nightfighters and inflict disastrous losses upon even the largest raids. Harris also failed to appreciate that equipping all the Pathfinder Lancasters with H2S radar –

an active emitter – would increase the vulnerability of his bombers and reduce the chances for success in a protracted campaign.

As more than 700 RAF bombers approached Berlin on the night of 23/24 August, the Luftwaffe scrambled 200+ nightfighter crews to defend the capital. This time, the Germans were able to deduce very quickly that Berlin was the target and they were able to mass the bulk of their fighters at nearby radio beacons. As the Pathfinders approached Berlin, using H2S radar to find landmarks on the ground, the Bf 110s pounced on them. A few German nightfighters were equipped with the new FuG 350 *Naxos* radar-warning receiver built by Telefunken, which enabled them to home in on H2S emissions.

Sqn Ldr Charles Lofthouse, flying a Pathfinder Lancaster from No. 7 Sqn, never saw what hit his aircraft:

> I saw a great, bright 'whoosh' of tracer come past the cockpit on the port side. I don't suppose anyone saw the attacking aeroplane – the gunners must have been blinded by the searchlights. This coloured tracer just raced by us, and all the damage was on the port side. The wings and engines were badly hit.

However, not all the Lancasters were easy kills. Leutnant Peter Spoden, a Bf 110 pilot from II./NJG 5, attacked a bomber over Berlin but he could not close in for a kill because 'he was corkscrewing, but very cleverly, making abrupt turns, not regularly according to the manual, and that saved him.'[3] Bomber Command succeeded in hitting Berlin, but at an unacceptable cost of 8.7 per cent losses. Twenty Lancasters were lost against five Bf 110s, although once other bomber losses were factored in, the *Nachtjagd* still enjoyed a 10-to-1 exchange rate.

Harris continued attacking Berlin, with 18 more raids over the next six months. He used the bomber stream tactic throughout the Battle of Berlin, even though *Himmelbett* had been rendered obsolete. Yet the bomber stream presented the *Nachtjagd* with a target-rich environment, particularly when it was obvious that Berlin was the target again and again. If the Bf 110s found the bomber stream, they could inflict far more damage than before, since the Lancasters were packed in so closely together. Throughout the Battle of Berlin, Harris' forces rarely enjoyed any kind of tactical surprise or technical advantage, and suffered accordingly. Now that Harris finally had his Main Force of more than 700 heavy bombers, he wanted to mass them against a single target to achieve maximum effect, but this preference militated against surprise and thus favoured the defenders. During the first three raids on Berlin, Bomber Command lost 125 bombers (including 50 Lancasters) and 988 aircrew in order to kill 1,282 German civilians. All three raids suffered a loss rate of more than six per cent, which threatened to castrate Bomber Command if it continued. In contrast, the *Nachtjagd* lost only ten nightfighters, including six Bf 110s, and had just five aircrew killed.

Both sides were working hard to field electronic devices that could tip the aerial war over Germany in their favour. Telefunken was able to introduce the improved FuG 220 *Lichtenstein* SN-2 radar, which was impervious to *Window*, although only small numbers of Bf 110s were equipped with it during the Battle of Berlin. Martini was also striving to deploy a new generation of ground-based early warning radars that were more resistant

---

3 Middlebrook, *The Berlin Raids*, p. 52

From the summer of 1943, the Luftwaffe was forced to employ valuable Bf 110 *Nachtjagd* units – such as NJG 3, seen here forming up while enemy aircraft circle behind them – against American daylight bomber formations. This not only caused much greater attrition of aircraft, but exhausted crews who then had to fly against the RAF at night. In daylight against massed bomber formations protected by USAAF fighters, the Bf 110 had no chance. (Bundesarchiv, Bild 101I-659-6436-31, Foto: Helmut Grosse)

to jamming. The use of the *Würzlaus* radar, which employed Doppler shift, significantly reduced false returns from *Window*.

Although German radars gradually regained their effectiveness in the autumn of 1943, the British also began a serious effort to target the *Nachtjagd's* VHF radio links. In October 1943, the British introduced Lancaster ABC aerial jammers and the ground-based *Corona* programme, both intended to disrupt the Luftwaffe's command and control over its Bf 110 nightfighters. German-speaking RAF and WAAF operators attempted to jam frequencies used by the Luftwaffe Y-stations, or impersonate JLOs and issue false orders directly to the Bf 110s. At least one Bf 110 nightfighter, flown by Leutnant Wilhelm Seuss, accepted a fake order from an RAF operator during a raid on Berlin and returned to his base.

The creation of No. 100 Group to conduct Radio Countermeasure (RCM) operations was a critical first step to increasing the survivability of Lancaster bombers over Germany, although the ongoing use of the bomber stream and H2S continued to contribute to heavy bomber losses. By the end of 1943 the *Nachtjagd* found that the RAF was jamming or disrupting most of its radio frequencies, which often made it more difficult to mass nightfighters against the bomber stream.

However, the British were less successful in their attempts to install radar devices in Lancasters that would warn crews of attacking German nightfighters. The *Monica* rearward-looking radar mounted beneath the rear turret provided too many false returns from other bombers, and most crews put little stock in its constant buzzing. The Germans evaluated *Monica* devices taken from the wrecks of shot-down Lancasters and quickly fielded the *Flensburg* radar warning receiver that homed in on *Monica*. A modification of the H2S radar known as *Fishpond* was introduced in November, but this also did little to provide advance warning of nightfighter attacks.

Bomber Command also remained ignorant about the existence of either the SN-2 radar or *Schräge Musik*, even though a captured German technician revealed some details about them in December 1943. As so often happens with PoW interrogations, the information was not believed. Meanwhile, the Luftwaffe leadership was so impressed with the initial combat performance of the improvised *Schräge Musik* fighters that it authorised the weapon's widespread adoption. A substantial number of Bf 110G-4 nightfighters began to receive both the SN-2 radar and *Schräge Musik* in September 1943, greatly increasing their lethality.

Due to the heavy losses of the August-September raids, Harris decided to halt the Battle of Berlin for two months in order to make good this attrition. However, he found little relief at Mannheim, where he lost 31 Lancasters in two raids, or Hanover, where he lost 49 Lancasters in three raids. Of the 15 major Bomber Command raids conducted during the pause in the Battle of Berlin, Harris lost another 151 Lancasters – about one-third of his available force. His bombers sustained a five per cent or greater loss rate on six out of 15 of these raids, indicating that the *Nachtjagd* had recovered from the disruption caused by *Window*. In contrast, a raid by 343 Lancasters over Stuttgart on the night of 7/8 October, supported by jamming from Lancaster ABCs, suffered only a 1.2 per cent loss rate. When Luftwaffe C2 was disrupted by jamming, few Bf 110s ever got into the fight, which saved many a Lancaster crew. During this period, Harris and his staff also developed better diversionary tactics to attempt to hide the Main Force on raids, but the Germans were quick to note that the RAF typically only used scarce H2S-equipped Pathfinders on actual targets. Detection of a mass of H2S signals usually identified Bomber Command's main effort and attracted the nightfighters.

The decision to equip a large number of Lancasters with H2S ground-mapping radar – the hump on the aft, lower fuselage of this late-war aircraft, which also has an AGLT – was done for the sake of improving bombing accuracy. However, it deprived the Lancaster of a means of defending itself against attacks from below and helped the Bf 110s to find the bombers from up to 100km away via the *Naxos* passive radar detector. (Imperial War Museum, E (MOS) 1403)

Harris resumed the Battle of Berlin in mid-November 1943, hoping that the long nights and miserable winter weather would shield his bombers from the German nightfighters. On 7 December he bombastically claimed that he could induce a German collapse with just 15,000 more Lancaster sorties over Berlin and other key cities. While the winter weather certainly had an impact on the battle, causing large numbers of non-combat crashes on both sides, Harris' hopes that the nightfighters would not be effective in poor weather proved illusory. On 16/17 December, Oberleutnant Heinz-Wolfgang Schnaufer from 12./NJG 1 gave a demonstration of the *Nachtjagd's* all-weather capabilities when he took off despite fog and severe icing and used his Bf 110G-4 equipped with SN-2 radar and *Schräge Musik* to shoot down four Lancasters. However, Schnaufer had great difficulty in finding his way home, and after landing said that he 'never again would take off in such conditions'. Another Bf 110 pilot was less lucky that night and crashed – a not unusual event for both sides in winter night combat. That same night Bomber Command also lost 32 Lancasters due to the poor weather. The *Nachtjagd* learned that only the most skilled pilots could operate on the worst winter nights, but this also meant that the nightfighters encountered by Bomber Command during this period were more likely to be flown by aces. In eight raids on Berlin between 18 November and 30 December, Harris lost 206 Lancasters – more than 40 per cent of his frontline strength. Stirling losses were so heavy that Harris decided to retire the surviving examples of the Short bomber from frontline service, as well as some of the older Halifaxes, which meant that the remainder of the battle would rest primarily on the shoulders of the Lancaster crews. During the same period, NJG 5, the main *Nachtjagd* unit defending Berlin, lost 14 Bf 110s in combat and another 12 in accidents – about one-third of its strength.

After a brief rest over Christmas, Bomber Command returned to Berlin in full force in January 1944. However, the *Nachtjagd* finally had enough nightfighters equipped with the new SN-2 radar to initiate the *Zahme Sau* tactic, which sought to attack aircraft

all along the bomber stream, not just at the target. This new tactic increased the opportunities for interception – leading to greater RAF losses – while reducing the chances that *Nachtjagd* fighters would be shot down by friendly flak near the target. Six more RAF raids on Berlin in January 1944 resulted in the loss of 152 Lancasters, and five of six raids suffered a six per cent loss rate or greater. Bomber Command had more Lancasters shot down in January 1944 than in any other month of the war and losses actually exceeded production for that month. One rising Bf 110G-4 pilot, Oberleutnant Paul Zorner of 8./NJG 3, shot down 22 Lancasters during the course of the

The RAF Y Service established *Corona* in Britain to disrupt Luftwaffe communications between ground controllers and circling Bf 110s. Using a captured German FuG 10 transmitter (centre), a German-speaking RAF WAAF flight sergeant is listening to Luftwaffe radio traffic and trying to issue false instructions to the Bf 110s. The phonograph was also used to play loud music to drown out German communications. (Imperial War Museum, CH 16682)

winter battles. Once in the bomber stream, a skilled pilot like Zorner or Schnaufer could decimate a flight of bombers in a matter of minutes. One Lancaster crewman described the sudden violence of a German *Schräge Musik* attack on his flight in January 1944:

The first indication of the nightfighter's presence was a stream of tracer from below our aircraft, port quarter. The target was a Lancaster flying some 100ft higher than us, on the same heading as our aircraft and located approximately 50 yards off our port bow. In less than two seconds both wing tanks of the Lancaster were ablaze. The nightfighter was still not seen by our rear gunner. A second attack was made almost simultaneously by the nightfighter on a Lancaster that was also some 100ft above our altitude and on the same heading, but off our starboard bow, at a distance of approximately 50 yards. The fate of the second Lancaster was exactly the same – both wings ablaze. The sky was now like day.

A Lancaster Airborne Cigar (ABC) from No. 101 Sqn drops a 4,000lb "cookie" and incendiaries over the Ruhr during a daylight raid on 14 October 1944. The creation of a specialised Lancaster electronic warfare squadron was a major step toward countering the effectiveness of the SN-2 radar-equipped Bf 110G-4 employing the *Nachtjagd's Zahme Sau* tactics. (Imperial War Museum, CL 1404)

This attack also originated from below and astern of our aircraft. The fighter was still not seen by either myself in the mid-upper turret or our rear gunner. A silver Messerschmitt then suddenly appeared immediately below the fuselage of our aircraft, slightly off our starboard beam, and some 20ft below our altitude. I immediately took action to engage him with my own guns, but he was too close and I was unable to depress my weapons sufficiently to bring his aircraft into my range of fire.[4]

Although Bomber Command increased its Mosquito Intruder flights in support of missions, and equipped the aircraft with the *Serrate* radar, which homed in on FuG 202 emissions, the *Serrate* could not detect the SN-2 radar. However, the Luftwaffe did a better job of keeping the Bf 110 pilots informed about enemy technology, and they were briefed about the *Monica* rearward looking radar appearing on Lancasters. Unteroffizier Otto Kutzner, a Bf 110G-4 pilot from 5./NJG 3, described his more cautious stalking of Lancasters near Berlin:

I believed that the bombers had equipment that warned them if a nightfighter was behind them so I didn't use my radar, but went searching for them in the area above where the markers were falling. It wasn't long before I spotted one. First, it was just a dark shadow but, when I came up behind it, I could see the eight exhausts and I recognised it as a Lancaster by the two egg-shaped tail fins. He never saw me – he just flew straight on.

Every pilot had his own method of attack. Mine was from directly behind so that I could put the tail gunner out of action to start with. I made sure I was in exactly the right position, at a range of about 50m, with at least the two outer engines in my gunsight. I gave it two bursts with my four cannons – a mixture of tracer and armour-piercing incendiary – all around the tail. The tail gunner must have been hit, for he never fired back. The tail began to burn and I think the ammunition for the tail turret exploded. I didn't watch it anymore because I wanted to look for another bomber, but my crew watched the Lancaster crash on the ground somewhere north of Berlin.[5]

Some RAF squadrons tried to keep their losses down by smart tactics. Gp Capt John H. Searby, who had been the Master Bomber on the Peenemünde Raid, instructed his Lancaster pilots in No. 83 Sqn to bank and weave continuously while over enemy territory, which made it more difficult for a nightfighter to target the aircraft. A Bf 110 pilot reported encountering a Lancaster that weaved and corkscrewed for 45 minutes, preventing him from attacking before he ran low on fuel and had to break off. Losses in No. 83 Sqn dropped and morale was no doubt improved. However, Searby was succeeded in command by Wg Cdr William Abercromby, who had different priorities and decided to discontinue these evasive tactics. Shortly thereafter Abercromby led his unit in a raid on Berlin, but his non-weaving Lancaster was blasted out of the sky by a Bf 110 shortly after crossing the Dutch coast.

Some Lancaster ABCs carried this electronic warfare package, known as *Jostle*. This airborne jamming device was intended to disrupt communications between the Luftwaffe Y-Stations and orbiting Bf 110s. RAF jamming became so effective by mid-1944 that the *Nachtjagd* was forced to use numerous work-arounds, such as the use of civilian radio broadcasts and coloured signals on the ground. (Imperial War Museum, CH 16683)

4 Middlebrook, *Berlin*, p. 206
5 Middlebrook, *Berlin*, p. 252

ENGAGING THE ENEMY

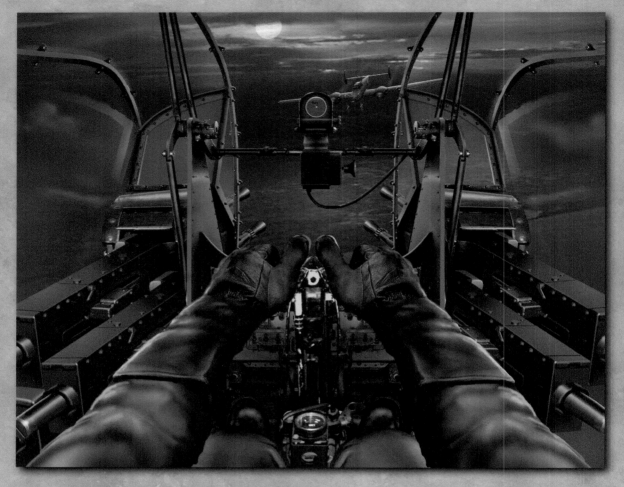

The only defensive armament aboard the Lancaster that could realistically engage a Bf 110 *Nachtjäger* was the rear FN 20 turret, with its four 0.303in. Browning machine guns. Each of the Brownings had 1,200 rounds of ammunition — enough for 60 seconds of firing, although bursts of two to three seconds were typical. A standard ammunition load was ten per cent tracer, 60 per cent armour-piercing and 30 per cent incendiary. However, the odds of a Lancaster rear gunner even sighting, never mind successfully engaging, an attacking Bf 110 at night were poor. After the war, surviving German *Nachtjagd* pilots reported that 80 per cent of the bombers they attacked never returned fire.

On long penetration flights over Germany, the rear gunners suffered badly from cold and had great difficulty maintaining alertness on missions that lasted six to eight hours. Rear gunners who dozed off or became inattentive risked their entire aircraft to stalking *Nachtjagd*. Yet, on occasion, less experienced German pilots either opened fire too far away or conducted sloppy approaches, thereby alerting the Lancaster crew.

The Brownings were harmonised at 229m, and the gunner controlled the turret with a twin-handled control column in the centre, which could turn the turret or elevate/depress the guns. The gunner used an illuminated Barr & Stroud Mk III reflector gunsight to aim his weapons, placing an orange dot on the enemy's fuselage. In this case, the gunner has a momentary deflection shot as the Bf 110 races past, scoring hits on its port engine. The 0.303in. rounds lacked penetrative power, which made it difficult to shoot down armoured Bf 110s. Yet most *Nachtjäger* would break off attacks if they received return fire, so a successful engagement did not necessarily require destroying the Bf 110.

Harris concluded the Battle of Berlin in March 1944, having failed to bring the Third Reich to its knees as he had boasted. Instead, months of attacks against a heavily defended target had nearly broken Bomber Command. The Battle of Berlin had cost the RAF 643 bombers, including 489 Lancasters, and 4,340 aircrew. The elite Pathfinder force was particularly decimated due to the tendency of its H2S radars to attract nightfighter attacks. Considering that Bomber Command dropped more than 33,000 tons of bombs on Berlin during the battle, it was also quite an achievement for the *Nachtjagd* to keep the death toll on the ground down to 10,305. There was no repeat of Hamburg.

Throughout the battle, Bomber Command regularly suffered loss rates of six per cent or more on raids, which caused morale among many Lancaster crews to sag. At this rate, very few would survive their 25-mission tour of duty. Furthermore, Harris knew that even with the emphasis Britain placed on heavy bomber construction, he could not replace these losses in the long run, and he was forced to suspend attacks on Berlin. However, *Nachtjagd* losses during the Battle of Berlin were significant, with NJG 5 losing more than 100+ Bf 110s from all causes.

In the later stages of the Battle of Berlin, Harris mounted major raids against other German cities, and introduced more sophisticated diversionary tactics in order to prevent the *Nachtjagd* from zeroing in on the bomber stream. In raids against Schweinfurt and Augsburg in February 1944, the Main Force was split into two waves separated by a two-hour interval, which succeeded in confusing the *Nachtjagd* enough to reduce bomber casualties to less than five per cent. However, the *Nachtjagd* quickly learned to compensate for this tactic, and when it was tried again over Stuttgart on 15/16 March, 27 Lancasters were shot down. Sometimes Bomber Command's diversionary raids using Mosquito light bombers succeeded in fooling the *Nachtjagd* long enough for the Lancaster Main Force to bomb its targets unmolested, but the norm was that most raids over Germany throughout the winter of 1943/44 suffered a four to five per cent casualty rate, which was nearly as bad as the Battle of Berlin.

As spring 1944 approached, Harris knew that he would soon be forced to divert Bomber Command to support the D-Day invasion by attacking targets in France. Since he regarded invasion support as a wasteful diversion from his main task of wrecking German cities, he stepped up his raids over Germany in March-May 1944. On the night of 30/31 March, Harris sent 795 bombers, including 572 Lancasters, to bomb Nurnberg. The attack was very poorly planned since it occurred on a night with bright moonlight and no cloud cover, so the bomber stream was easily detected. The Luftwaffe signal service proved unusually adept at identifying radio and H2S radar emissions from the raiding group while it was still over England, which gave the *Nachtjagd* plenty of advance warning.

The 3. *Jagddivision* at Deelen rapidly identified the Main Force from a diversionary formation sent over the North Sea and quickly vectored about 150 nightfighters towards the approaching RAF bomber stream. The aerial battle proper began as the stream passed south of the Ruhr and quickly turned into a slaughter, with nightfighters scoring multiple kills in rapid succession. *Schräge Musik*-equipped Bf 110s proved particularly lethal. Despite sending out 19 *Serrate* Mosquitoes to disrupt the nightfighters, they failed in their mission because they could not detect the new SN-2 radar. Similarly, No. 101 Sqn despatched 26 Lancaster ABCs to support the raid, but

six were shot down. Furthermore, German pilots had learned that the British briefly stopped their jamming every hour for a few minutes to receive weather updates, and the *Nachtjagd* used these precious minutes of un-jammed time to coordinate their nightfighter groups. One Lancaster from No. 166 Sqn was badly shot up by an attacking Bf 110G-4 but its rear gunner managed to destroy the nightfighter – the only one lost that night. Oberleutnant Martin Becker, who was involved in intercepting the bomber stream, recalled, 'They seemed to be lining up to be shot down. I just had to stop after the seventh one. I was sick of the killing'. All told, Bomber Command had 95 bombers shot down, 64 of which were Lancasters – a total of nearly 12 per cent of the raiding force. Some 721 crewmen were also lost, as opposed to just 11 for the *Nachtjagd*. Even worse, most of the raiding force missed Nurnberg completely and inflicted only token damage on the target.

The Nurnberg Raid of 30/31 March was a disaster for Bomber Command, and it graphically demonstrated that the *Nachtjagd* was actually growing stronger, not weaker. RAF raids in April 1944 cost another 112 Lancasters, particularly in punishing operations over Schweinfurt and Friedrichshafen. Although Harris would not admit defeat, he finally recognised the tactical dominance of the German nightfighters in a letter to the Air Ministry on 7 April 1944:

> The strength of the German defences would in time reach a point at which night-bombing
> attacks by existing methods and types of heavy bomber would involve percentage casualty
> rates which could not in the long run be sustained. We have not yet reached that point,
> but tactical innovations which have so far postponed it are now practically exhausted.

The approaching D-Day invasion allowed Harris to cut back on operations over Germany for a time in order to concentrate on targets in France, which promised to reduce bomber losses. On the night of 3/4 May, 346 Lancasters from Nos. 1 and 5 Groups took off to bomb the German panzer training school at Mailly-le-Camp, south of Rheims. It was expected to be an 'easy' operation, in clear weather. However, this supposedly easy raid turned into a 'shambles' when an American Armed Forces radio network broadcast of 'Deep in the Heart of Texas' began drowning out the Master Bomber's instructions to the Main Force. Awaiting the order to attack, hundreds of Lancasters circled 15 miles from Mailly-le-Camp. Now it was the RAF's turn to experience the disruptive effects of jamming upon night operations, and the *Nachtjagd* swung into action with Bf 110s from six different *Gruppen*. Plt Off Russell 'Rusty' Waughman, flying a Lancaster ABC from No. 101 Sqn remembered:

Eleven minutes before bombing we were attacked by a fighter. By 'corkscrewing' we evaded the attack. My gunners, in whom I had every confidence, were excellent. When they shouted 'corkscrew', I did not wait to ask 'why'. If I had it would have been too late and we would have had cannon shells up our rear end! The Main Force was held at the assembly point, waiting for the Master Bombers to make an accurate marking of the target. At the assembly point things hotted up quickly. There was a lot of German fighter activity, and main-force aircraft were seen being shot down. There was considerable interference on the R/T from an American broadcast station. This made it very difficult, if not impossible, for the Main Force to hear any instructions from the 'Master of Ceremonies'. There was a lot of tension, I hesitate to say panic, at the assembly point.

Plt Off Waughman bombed the target and made it home, but four of the 21 Lancaster ABCs in his squadron did not. Many Bomber Command pilots described the mission as a 'nightfighter massacre'. All told, 42 Lancasters were shot down in less than an hour – possibly as many as 36 by Bf 110G-4 nightfighters – amounting to an 11.6 per cent loss rate. Hauptmann Helmut Bergmann, a Bf 110G-4 pilot from 8./NJG 4, shot down five of the Lancasters. The Mailly-le-Camp fiasco was a shock to Lancaster crews, particularly coming so soon after heavy losses over Berlin and Nurnberg. Subsequent raids on the Ruhr in May and June continued the prevailing trend, with most night operations suffering five per cent or greater losses. A raid on the synthetic oil plant at Wesseling, in the Ruhr, on 21/22 June encountered another well-coordinated nightfighter ambush that resulted in 37 of 133 Lancasters being shot down – a 27.8 per cent loss rate.

Oddly, Harris continued with night raids even though it would have been far safer to transition to day raids at this point due to Allied air superiority. The one exception to continued heavy Lancaster losses at the hands of Bf 110 nightfighters was a raid on Kiel on 23/24 July in which new electronic warfare techniques completely baffled the *Nachtjagd*. Bomber Command established a *Mandrel* jamming screen over the North Sea that prevented German radar from seeing the Main Force forming up, and the bombers appeared suddenly from the sea. Heavy jamming also disrupted Luftwaffe C2 communications. Consequently, only four of 519 Lancasters were lost.

Most British histories of Bomber Command choose to emphasise that bomber losses in night raids dropped from 3.5 per cent in 1943 to two per cent in 1944, suggesting that RAF bombers had gained a decisive edge in the air war over Germany. In fact, it is more pertinent to note that 1,041 Lancasters were lost on operational sorties in the first six months of 1944, which was equivalent to the loss of 70 per cent of all Lancasters built in this period. When aircraft written off in accidents and non-combat losses are factored in as well, Bomber Command lost the equivalent of 94 per cent of the Lancasters built in the first half of 1944. Simply put, the *Nachtjagd* – particularly the Bf 110G-4s with SN-2 radar and *Schräge Musik* – were shooting down Lancasters almost as fast as the British could build them.

The RAF's failure to learn about the capabilities of the SN-2 and *Schräge Musik* for more than eight months after the *Nachtjagd* began using them left the Lancaster crews virtually defenceless during the most intense phase of the bombing of Germany. During this period, from June 1943 to July 1944, the Bf 110 clearly bested the Lancasters in their aerial duels over Germany.

OVERLEAF

On the night of 30/31 March 1944, Bomber Command sent 725 heavy bombers to attack the city of Nurnberg, in Bavaria, including 26 Lancasters from No. 101 Sqn that were fitted with ABC radio jamming equipment. However, no amount of jamming could hide the bomber stream in the bright moonlight. Oberleutnant Wilhelm Seuss from 11./NJG 5 was flying one of the Bf 110G-4s that intercepted the bombers. He did not need his SN-2 radar to spot his targets, whose contrails were illuminated in the bright moonlight. Seuss infiltrated the bomber stream and used his *Schräge Musik* to shoot down two Lancasters in four minutes. He then found Lancaster ABC "SR-J" flown by Flt Sgt Clyde Harnish (RCAF) of No. 101 Sqn. Seuss got underneath the Lancaster, but when he pushed the trigger only two rounds fired before his ammunition was exhausted. Harnish saw the tracer fire and put the Lancaster into a corkscrew manoeuvre, diving rapidly. Seuss, however, was able to stay with him while his *bordfunker* put a new ammunition drum in the upward-firing cannon. After three minutes, Harnish assumed that he had lost the nightfighter and resumed level flight, but by this point Seuss' cannons had been reloaded. The German aimed for the port wing as he was trained, but as the first rounds impacted Harnish dived again, causing Seuss' *Schräge Musik* fire to hit the bomb-bay and starboard wing as well. Seuss turned away as Harnish's bomber fell in flames and managed to shoot down one more Lancaster before returning to base. Harnish died in the crash, but four of eight crewmen survived.

The brand new, battle-damaged, Bf 110G-4/R3 from III./NJG 6 (flown by 34-victory ace Oberleutnant Wilhelm Johnen – note the victory markings on the fighter's fin) that accidentally landed on Dübendorf airfield, Switzerland, on 27 April 1944 was a lucky break for Allied intelligence. The opportunistic Swiss destroyed the aircraft after horse-trading with the Germans, but not before they had allowed Allied diplomats to learn the frequency of the FuG 220 SN-2 radar and confirmed the existence of upward-firing *Schräge Musik* cannons. (via Jerry Scutts)

Despite routinely inflicting grievous losses on Lancaster raids, the Bf 110's days were numbered by the summer of 1944. American bomber raids on the German synthetic oil plants in March 1944 greatly reduced the amount of fuel available for the Luftwaffe, which affected both training and operations for the Bf 110 force. Even worse, the accidental landing in Switzerland of a Bf 110G-4 damaged by return fire from a Lancaster bomber in April, followed by a lost Ju 88 nightfighter landing in England in July, revealed to the RAF the frequency of the SN-2 radar and confirmed the existence of *Schräge Musik*. This knowledge enabled the RAF to alter the Mosquito nightfighter's *Serrate* receiver to detect SN-2 emissions, which led to more Bf 110 losses from British intruder missions. The captured Ju 88 was fitted with a FuG 227 *Flensburg* radar warning receiver, which the British found could detect *Monica* emissions, so that system was immediately pulled off Lancasters.

Even before the invasion of France, USAAF fighters had begun attacking NJG 4 bases in France, and eventually NJG 1 bases in Holland and Belgium were also frequently strafed. The triumph of the nightfighter massacre at Mailly-le-Camp was followed by the massacre of the nightfighters themselves in May-July 1944, with almost 336 Bf 110s being lost in just three months. On 15 August almost 600 Lancasters conducted daylight attacks on NJG 1's airfields in Belgium and Holland, wrecking these bases and forcing NJG 1 to relocate back to airfields in the Ruhr. The German retreat from France and Belgium also hurt the *Nachtjagd* badly due to the loss of radar sites and other equipment. Before D-Day the Luftwaffe leadership had decided to phase out the Bf 110G-4 and convert *staffeln* to the improved Ju 88G-6 nightfighter, and this process was accelerated in September. The number of Bf 110-equipped *Nachtjagd gruppen* dropped from 16 in January 1944 to ten in December 1944 and just five by April 1945, but the aircraft remained in the fight to the finish.

Amazingly, Harris continued to fly night raids over Germany during the autumn and winter months, even though American bomber formations escorted by P-51s were often unopposed by Luftwaffe day fighters. By this point

By the autumn of 1944 Allied air supremacy had forced the *Nachtjagd* to disperse and camouflage its Bf 110s during daylight hours so as to evade strafing attacks. RAF Mosquito intruder operations also took a toll on Bf 110s using known *Nachtjagd* airfields. As the Luftwaffe's power faded, the German nightfighter force went from being the hunters to the hunted. (Author)

Bomber Command had honed night bombing to a fine art, and it was reluctant to shift back to the day bombing of major targets, although this reluctance continued to allow the *Nachtjagd's* Bf 110s to score against Lancasters. The *Nachtjagd* no longer had the strength or fuel to oppose all of Bomber Command's night raids, but when it did, RAF losses remained heavy. Some 467 Lancasters were lost on operations in the last four months of the war, which was only 1.1 per cent of those sortied, but 48 per cent of the Lancasters built during the same period.

Many of the great Lancaster and Bf 110 pilots lost their lives, even as the end was nearly in sight. In a bizarre twist of fate, Wg Cdr Guy Gibson, one of the most famous Lancaster pilots of World War II, is believed to have been shot down while acting as a Master Bomber on a raid on 19/20 September 1944. Gibson's Mosquito was apparently mistaken by a Lancaster rear turret gunner for a Ju 88 nightfighter over Holland and shot down. Unfortunately, fratricide was a fact of life for both sides in night combat, with a number of Lancasters and Bf 110s accidently shot down by their own side.

Although the RAF had fitted 0.50in. heavy machine gun-equipped FN 82 turrets to a few hundred Lancasters by the autumn of 1944, Bomber Command never developed an effective counter to *Schräge Musik*, which enabled those Bf 110G-4s equipped with it to remain lethal right up to the end. On 22 February 1945, Major Heinz-Wolfgang Schnaufer used *Schräge Musik* to shoot down seven Lancasters in just 19 minutes. He only broke off the action when his ammunition was exhausted. Schnaufer shot down another three Lancasters on 7 March 1945, these being his last victories before war's end. On the other hand, Bomber Command's electronic warfare continued to improve, and by early 1945 the RAF had the ability to jam even the SN-2 radar. A handful of *experten* like Schnaufer continued to use the Bf 110G-6 in final battles with Lancasters until April 1945, but the Messerschmitt fighter comprised only one-fifth of the *Nachtjagd's* strength in the final months of the war.

The other effort to improve Lancaster rearward defensive armament was the FN 82 turret, also fitted with two 0.50in. heavy machine guns. The bulbous device is the Automatic Gun-Laying Turret (AGLT) or 'Village Green', introduced in four Lancaster squadrons from October 1944. AGLT was an active radar that detected incoming nightfighters and automatically laid the 0.50in. machine guns on the target. (Imperial War Museum, MH 22160)

The shattered remains of a Lancaster bomber shot down over Germany by a Bf 110 nightfighter. More than 3,000 Lancasters were lost in bombing raids over Europe in 1942-45, with the largest proportion being shot down by Bf 110s. Lone *Zerstörer*, often flown by *experten*, were still able to shoot down multiple Lancasters in a single night right up to the last weeks of the war. (Author)

STATISTICS AND ANALYSIS

The story of Bomber Command's operations over Germany is usually told in terms of bomb tonnage dropped and German civilian deaths – which is how Harris viewed the campaign. Yet whether or not any Lancasters dropped bombs over Germany was just as irrelevant to the duel between the Lancaster and Bf 110 as whether any German bombers dropped ordnance on London was irrelevant to the duel between the He 111 and the Hurricane in the summer of 1940. Compounding the irrelevance, post-war surveys demonstrated that between 20 and 30 per cent of the bombs dropped by Lancasters failed to explode, and that night bombing accuracy remained sketchy until the last 12 months of the war.

A total of 6,924 Lancasters were built between October 1941 and May 1945 at an average cost of £32,000 each. Between March 1942 and May 1945, the Lancasters flew 156,000 sorties, or 41 per cent of Bomber Command's operational effort. A total of 3,249 Lancasters were lost in action and another 1,005 in training or non-combat accidents. Fully 58 per cent of the Lancasters built in 1941-45 were destroyed, which was the highest percentage loss of any RAF aircraft. Additionally, something like 25,000 RAF aircrew also died while serving in Lancasters. Britain decided to make the Lancaster the centrepiece in its war against the Third Reich and spent £2.78 billion on the strategic air offensive, representing 12 per cent of the UK's military expenditure in World War II. Unfortunately, the Lancasters proved unable to inflict sufficient damage upon Germany to be decisive.

As the top table opposite depicts, total Lancaster losses from all causes only exceeded production in one month, January 1944, although the figure for attrition

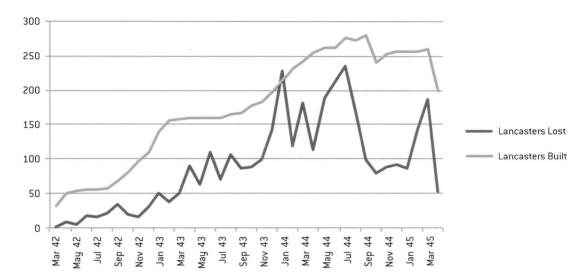

remained above 50 per cent for most of the war. The sortie loss rates compiled by the RAF concealed the fact that between mid-1942 and mid-1944, the Luftwaffe was shooting down at least half the bombers built each month – a catastrophic rate of loss.

Germany built just over 2,000 Bf 110 nightfighters between 1941-45, at an average cost of about £19,300 per aircraft. More than 800 were lost in combat and another 800 destroyed in training and accidents. When combined, these figures represent about 82 per cent of total production. Roughly 2,000 Bf 110 aircrew died as a result of combat losses and accidents. The table below indicates that Bf 110 nightfighter losses initially exceeded monthly production in September 1943, and this occurred several times in 1944.

In the three-year duel between Bf 110s and Lancasters, crews flying the German nightfigher succeeded in shooting down more than 1,500 Lancasters. Numerous Bf 110

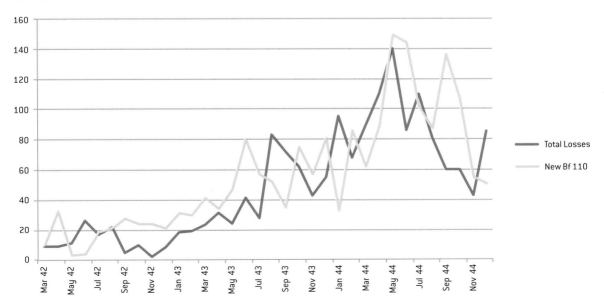

The two top-ranking fighter aces of the *Nachtjagd*, Oberleutnant Helmut Lent (left) and Hauptmann Heinz-Wolfgang Schnaufer, who between them destroyed a staggering 223 Allied aircraft – more than half of these were Lancasters. This photograph was taken before October 1944, when Lent was killed while serving as *Kommodore* of NJG 3. Schnaufer was *Kommandeur* of IV./NJG 1 at the time. (via Jerry Scutts)

pilots, including Schnaufer, Drewes, Werner Streib and Paul Zorner, shot down multiple Lancasters on a single night, which was a feat that few Luftwaffe day fighter pilots accomplished against American heavy bombers. Conversely, it is unclear how many Bf 110s were shot down by Lancasters, but available evidence indicates that exchange rates varied between five and twenty Lancasters downed for every Bf 110 destroyed. This suggests that Lancaster gunners accounted for perhaps 150 Bf 110s. Anecdotal evidence suggests that most of the Bf 110 pilots shot down by Lancasters were inexperienced. In strictly quantitative terms, both Bf 110 and Lancaster squadrons were badly bloodied in this protracted battle of attrition, but the Bf 110s almost always inflicted much greater damage on the bombers than they received. Stanley Baldwin was proved correct. The bomber did always get through, but not always at an acceptable price in terms of aircraft and aircrew lost, nor did they always achieve what was intended.

The Bf 110 versus Lancaster duel is also very interesting from a technological standpoint, as both sides adapted to each other's tactics and employed an increasingly complex array of electronic countermeasures. The role of intelligence was critical in the duel, with the capture of enemy technology leading to rapid shifts in combat advantage. British failures to appreciate German technical advances were the primary cause of the heavy Lancaster losses of 1943-44. Despite the Allies breaking the Luftwaffe Enigma codes, the *Nachtjagd* still managed to keep its best secrets under wraps. The Germans gained the initial advantage by developing the *Himmelbett* system and deploying Bf 110 nightfighters equipped with FuG 202 *Lichtenstein* radar, but this was neutralised by *Window*. The Germans regained the advantage by mounting improved SN-2 radars and *Schräge Musik* on selected Bf 110s, neither of which were ever completely countered by the RAF. Virtually all of the defensive measures installed in Lancasters – *Monica*, *Fishpond* and 0.50in. turrets – proved either ineffective or too late to reduce excessive losses from nightfighter attacks. Indeed, *Monica* actually led to greater Lancaster losses once the Bf 110s received *Flensburg* receivers to home in on the emissions put out by the system. It is clear that the most important measure introduced into the duel by Bomber Command was the jamming and electronic warfare conducted by the Lancaster ABCs and ground-based stations, which severely disrupted the Bf 110's all-important C2 and radio navigation linkages.

AFTERMATH

Even as the Third Reich crumbled into ruin in April 1945, the surviving Bf 110s remained an undefeated force. Whereas darkness protected the bombers in the early years of the war, by the end it was protecting the nightfighters from the depredations of Allied day fighters. The Luftwaffe gradually expanded its *Nachtjagd* capabilities in 1940-44 from non-existent to point defence of cities, to static zone defence and finally mobile area defence. However, the Bf 110 nightfighter force was hobbled by insufficient resources devoted to replacing lost pilots and aircraft. Avro's ability to build hundreds of Lancasters every month and the success of the EATS in producing replacement aircrew were critical factors in preventing Bomber Command from being defeated by the Bf 110 nightfighters in 1943.

The lop-sided losses suffered by the Lancaster squadrons in three years of nocturnal duels with the *Nachtjagd*'s Bf 110 *staffeln* were the logical result of a weapon system that was designed around a single characteristic – bombload. Yet it was not enough for the Lancaster to reach Berlin with a large bombload. The aircraft needed to survive and make multiple missions in order to justify the cost of its construction. Britain's commitment to heavy bombers and night strategic bombing became a very expensive obsession that was undermined by a failure to conduct realistic operational assessments in the critical early days of the Lancaster programme. Too much effort was focused on achieving maximum range and bombloads, without commensurate effort put into night navigation and defensive measures until failure became a very real possibility. In a tactical sense, the Bf 110G-4 with SN-2 radar and *Schräge Musik*, routinely decimated Lancaster raids at an exchange rate that Bomber Command could ill afford. Only the overall decline of the German military position and the failure to prioritise nightfighter production prevented the Bf 110s from demolishing Harris' Lancaster Main Force. Instead, increasingly fuel-starved Bf 110s ended up fighting an exhausting

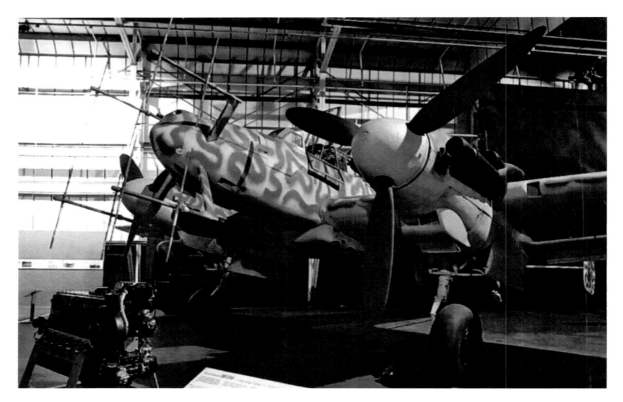

The only surviving Bf 110 nightfighter in the world today is G-4d/R-3 wk-nr 730301, located in the RAF Museum at Hendon, in northwest London. It was surrendered to the Allies at Grove airfield, in Denmark, at war's end and was subsequently sent to the UK for evaluation. The Bf 110's reputation was damaged by its early failure in the Battle of Britain, and then over-shadowed by more modern German aircraft introduced in 1941-45. However, Willy Messerschmitt's twin-engined fighter shot down thousands of Allied bombers and remained a threat that no Lancaster crew could ever ignore.

and futile holding action waiting for new, improved machines like the He 219 that never showed up in quantity.

The sad fact is that Harris had the weapon in hand to bomb Berlin with relative impunity – the de Havilland Mosquito. While its bomb load was inferior to the Lancaster's, the Mosquito's superior speed made it virtually invulnerable to the Bf 110 and Germany's other night defences. The Light Bomber Force, based upon the Mosquito, was the model for successful strategic night bombing, but Harris would not allow any reduction in his monthly bomb tonnage delivery statistics and would not allow the Mosquito to supplant the Lancaster.

FURTHER READING

BOOKS

Boiten, Theo E. W. and Martin W. Bowman, *Battles with the Nachtjagd* (Schiffer Publishing Ltd, 2006)

Bushby, J. R., 'British Bomber Defence 1939-1945,' *The Putnam Aeronautical Review* No. 7, September 1990, pp. 173-182

Dyson, Freeman, *Disturbing the Universe* (Basic Books, 1979)

Foreman, John et al., *Luftwaffe Night Fighter Combat Claims 1939-1945* (Red Kite Books, 2004)

Hastings, Max, *Bomber Command* (Pan Books, 1999)

Hinchliffe, Peter, *The Other Battle – Luftwaffe Night Aces Versus Bomber Command* (Castle Books, 2001)

Jucker, Hans H., *German FuG 202/FuG 220 Lichtenstein airborne radars*

McKinstry, Leo, *Lancaster* (John Murray Publishers, 2009)

Middlebrook, Martin, *The Bomber Command War Diaries* (Midland Publishing, 1996)

Middlebrook, Martin, *The Battle of Hamburg* (Cassell & Co., 2000)

Middlebrook, Martin, *The Peenemunde Raid* (Cassell & Co., 2000)

Middlebrook, Martin, *The Berlin Raids* (Cassell & Co., 2000)

Penrose, Harald, *Architect of Wings – A Biography of Roy Chadwick, Designer of the Lancaster Bomber* (Airlife Publishing Ltd., 1985)

Sinnott, Colin S., *The RAF and Aircraft Design – Air Staff Operational Requirements 1923-1939* (Routledge, 2001)

WEBSITES

http://www.lancaster-archive.com
http://www.deutscheluftwaffe.de/
http://www.ww2.dk/
http://www.luftwaffe.cz/nacht.html
http://www.gyges.dk/index.htm
http://www.pauke-pauke.net/pauke/index.php/en

INDEX